IN REAL LIFE

IN REAL LIFE

SEARCHING FOR CONNECTION
IN HIGH-TECH TIMES

JON MITCHELL

PARALLAX
PRESS

Parallax Press
P.O. Box 7355
Berkeley, California 94707
parallax.org

Parallax Press is the publishing division
of the Unified Buddhist Church, Inc.
© 2015 by Jon Mitchell

Cover and text design by Jess Morphew
Cover images: Eye © Marish / Shutterstock;
Background © Melamory / Shutterstock
Author photo © John Curley

Library of Congress Cataloging-in-Publication Data

Mitchell, Jon P., 1987-
  In real life : searching for connection in high-tech times / Jon P.
Mitchell.
      pages cm
    ISBN 978-1-937006-90-7 (paperback)
    1. Self-actualization (Psychology) 2. Human-computer interaction.
3.
Success. I. Title.
   BF637.S4M566 2015
   155.9--dc23

Printed on 100% post-consumer
waste recycled paper

1 2 3 4 5 / 19 18 17 16 15

To all my teachers

CONTENTS

INTRODUCTION

This is a book about the present moment and what we can do right now to improve our relationship with technology. This isn't a "pro-technology" or "anti-technology" book. Being "pro-" or "anti-technology" is like being "pro-" or "anti-air." It doesn't matter how we feel about technology; it's there, and it will always be there. Maybe the notions of "pro-technology" and "anti-technology" exist because we don't have a clear understanding of what technology is.

Technology, as defined in the Merriam-Webster Dictionary, is "a machine, piece of equipment, or method that is created using science and engineering." Mainstream tech media, where I worked as a journalist, describes technology as an environmental and economic force that drives human progress and standards of living. Regardless of your opinion about it or how you define it, chances are you're using technology in some way every day, so it might be beneficial to have an intentional relationship with it and know more about what you're doing.

As a technology writer, I've been carefully observing one of the fastest, broadest revolutions in human history: the advent of mobile, networked computing. I think out loud about it and try to help others understand it as I've tried to understand it myself. But my exploration of technology has always had a spiritual motivation. Technology provides humankind with a "how," but spirituality provides a "why," which I believe must come first. After exploring different approaches to creating a more intentional relationship with the new tools we use, I offer this simple manifesto: Let's keep our technology in tune with the human heart so that it amplifies the best things in our nature.

SPIRITUAL WORK, SPIRITUAL JOBS

The purpose of technology is to do work for us. In the most basic, physical sense, any force acting on any body is doing work. The reason we invent any technology is to increase our impact on the world. In that sense, work is the underlying subject of every tech story.

In the economies of human societies, work is usually discussed on an abstract level. We also use the word "work" to describe the activities people do for monetary compensation. The market places a value on various forms of labor, denominated in money, and people try to find a job doing one of these kinds of work, so they can make money and survive. In high-tech societies, technology stories are largely concerned with work in this sense, showing how new inventions and innovations can make people and companies be more productive, efficient, and profitable. This isn't that kind of story. Rather, I'm concerned with work of the highest human order. How can technology enable us, as individuals and communities, to do the work of being a good person? This is the kind of work we can be doing all the time, whether in our jobs, with our friends and families, with strangers on the street, in the airport, on the highway, at the hospital, anywhere. It's the work of being present to the needs and wants of other people—and ourselves, too—so we can help each other thrive and be happy.

The meaning of words is shaped by our upbringing, our religious and cultural traditions, and our social environments. Religions and moral philosophies are defined and distinguished from one another by the different values and practices they prescribe for a good life. But we have to translate across these lines in order to live together as neighbors. In a diverse and deeply interconnected society, there are best practices we can share to help us do our spiritual work, however we define it for ourselves.

We have created technology to help us do our work, but it can't help us if we don't know what our true work is. "The computer will do anything within its abilities, but it will do nothing unless commanded to do so," the designer and computer scientist John Maeda said.[1] What will we command the computer to do? This turns out to be a profoundly ethical question.

The task before us is to identify the qualities of good spiritual work for ourselves, as well as to isolate what is negative or unwholesome—the spiritually harmful kinds of work in which we may engage as we tread our path through the world. To know what our work is requires an ongoing evaluation and, I would argue, mindfulness meditation. A stereotype of meditation is that it involves sitting and staring into space, thinking of nothing. I define mindfulness meditation as an ongoing project of discovering greater awareness of our true nature and the nature of the moment that we're in. We then can use these insights to help us define our purpose and, from that purpose, our work.

Of course the moment we're facing changes all the time, and so does the technology around us. Mindfulness needs to be a daily practice so that we get in the habit of discerning—in the constant stream of new technology and distractions coming at us—what is helpful and what is not.

This can be an uphill battle. The technologies we use day to day are sometimes not designed to help us do good work. Indeed, some of them are designed to distract us. While those distractions are formidable, the language of technology is always reasonable and transparent enough for us to understand. Once we understand why some technologies are designed for distraction, we will be empowered to create better, more helpful tools.

"Almost every project could be done better, and an infinite quantity of information is now available that could make that happen," wrote David Allen in his seminal productivity bible, *Getting Things Done*.[2] That goal poses a risk of overwhelming our efforts. But the way out of this dilemma isn't to avoid technology and information, but to find and develop ways of using them to our advantage. As Allen wrote in another book, *Ready for Anything*, "Sometimes the biggest gain in productive energy will come from cleaning the cobwebs, dealing with old business, and clearing the desks—cutting loose debris that's impeding forward motion."[3]

Even technologies that are designed to distract and entertain can be used for higher purposes. The kinds of distractions provided by the Internet often also have the function of connecting us with other people. That connection can be used to accomplish a higher purpose, as any human connection can. It just takes conscious intention and presence of mind. A spiritual relationship with technology is one in which we, the users, can apply technological powers for their most beneficial purposes. The work of building supportive community, deepening our connection to the world around us, and doing good in the world can be amplified to amazing scale with the power of modern technology.

There are risks, of course, and pitfalls along the way.

A mindfulness practice, which I define as regular and intentional time set aside to strengthen our awareness, is a necessary foundation for building a healthy relationship with technology. If we are subject to its tempting distractions, we'll lose time we could spend on more beneficial work. If we act in the world without introspection, technology will only amplify our recklessness.

We've created technologies to help us, and if our life is to have meaning and value for us then the tools we use need to have meaning as well. If we want to use technology for good, then we have to give it the right jobs to do.

<<<< WORK AND PURPOSE >>>>

"One of the more embarrassing and self-indulgent challenges of our time is the task of remembering how to concentrate," Alain de Botton writes in his brief, beautiful essay "On Distraction." He observes that high technology has brought along "an unparalleled assault on our capacity to fix our minds steadily on anything. To sit still and think, without succumbing to an anxious reach for a machine, has become almost impossible."[4] The need for clarity in communication, to tell the computer we need to pay attention, is also a spiritual problem. Spiritual practice might seem like it belongs in a different book from Internet habits, but that's not so. When we observe the world, we see that everything is connected, and this is true too of the relationship between computers and people.

Maybe it's uncomfortable to think about a computer in this way. It's an inanimate object. It has a power button; you can turn it on and off. Perhaps you could say it has a kind of intelligence—but it's not human, it's not an animal—so how can it have a relationship with a person?

It may sound too intimate. But we *are* intimate with computers. We communicate with them through touch. Sometimes we talk to them. Sometimes we gaze at them. Computers are there for us during intimate moments. They facilitate our human relationships. They teach us wonderful things about our world. They can monitor and protect our health. They can help us with our hardest work.

Computers also offer us endless distractions. They indulge our vanity and our laziness. They disembody us, dehumanize us, and dehumanize others in our eyes. But they can only do that if we have told and allowed them to do so. We've given them bad jobs to do. We've given them instructions that aren't in alignment with our best nature and our deepest needs. That's why it's important to know what jobs to give our computers. We can stay on track by keeping in mind such questions as: *What are you doing today? What are you doing in this moment?*

We all keep some kind of list—whether paper, digital, or mental—of what we have to do. If a task is on the list it doesn't necessarily mean we'll do it today. Some tasks can't be avoided, some are better done in days or weeks to come, still others can be postponed or pushed guiltily to tomorrow.

What are you doing in this moment? is a question we can ask ourselves from the moment we wake up. We want to have a good answer. It gives us a sense of purpose to know what we're doing. We can lose our worries and doubts in action. When we know what to do, we are part of an active world. When we don't know what to do, we feel alone. But we are not alone. There is something else that can help us figure out what to do. Our computer.

The relationship between person and computer is not even a generation old. At first, the computers weren't capable of having a complex relationship with us. Now, they are. We're the ones out of our depth in this relationship now.

Computers have the simpler job in this relationship. They know what they want from us because we have told them. Therefore, it's important that first of all we know what we want from computers, so that we can give them the right instructions that will facilitate our focus on meaningful work. So our part is harder, because it means we have to know and understand what we want and need. If we program our computers to relate to us on any less substantial basis, they won't perform in accord with our wants and needs. When an ad is programmed to pop up and interrupt us while we're reading a friend's important message this isn't helpful, because in that moment we need to be present and focusing on our friend.

So far, in most computer-human relationships, we've asked computers to help us with the question: *What are you doing in this moment?* Computers help us remember what we're doing, they help us find new things to do, and they help us to do them. Sometimes computers are so helpful that they help us in opposing ways!

For example, a computer can help you remember what you're doing today by showing your tasks on a calendar. Then it can help you take the next step of writing a message to your team by opening a new application in a new window, allowing you to focus on what you want to write.

But maybe while you're writing, a friend sends you a message: "Want to get pizza for lunch?" Your computer receives that message, and it does exactly what it was told to do: it delivers the message to you right away. In fulfilling its purpose of helping you plan your day, it's now interrupting you. In doing so it may impede you from getting on with the task at hand. That's no help at all.

The computer is just doing what it's been asked to do. But it's helping you in two ways at the same time. Is that what you had wanted it to do? Do you and your computer have a communication problem? If so, then you need to figure out how to explain yourself better. That's the key to any healthy relationship. And again, to do that, you have to understand yourself. Is having single-pointed concentration at the times it's needed something that's important to you? It's probably important to everyone to some degree—and teachers of meditation would corroborate its benefit! So if we care about being present, aware, and purposeful, and not letting our mind wander too much, we shouldn't let technology get in the way. But we do.

Our relationship with computers is certainly not the same as our human relationships. For now, at least, computers are more like mindless servants than friends. They follow our instructions and do prodigious work. We may buy a computer or an app because of something we like about it, but ultimately our relationship with a computer and its software is defined by how well it does the jobs for which we've hired it.

How do we know what jobs to give our computers? Some of them are obvious. It's our computer's job to do hard math problems for us, to send and receive our email, or to help us browse the Internet. But when we're not careful, we give our computers bad jobs to do, perhaps unconsciously or by accident. Is it our computer's job to help us procrastinate in an addictive game? Is it our computer's job to make us feel insecure by browsing our exes' photos? It is if that's what we have told our computer to do.

If we want our technology to help us, we have to be more mindful managers. We have to hire the right tools for the right jobs. If you don't know what jobs you're hiring for, it can be helpful to ask: *What is your work?*

Your work is the impact you make on the world. Whether technology helps you or hinders you in that work is in your hands. Some work can be dry, boring, or even painful. So we should accept help. Technology is here to help us. That's the reason we created it. We just have to use it with awareness and intention so it can truly help us. When we're empowered with the right tools, work can be joyous, uplifting, satisfying, cathartic, and transformative. Doing work that inspires us and helps the world is key to transforming suffering and finding balance in our lives. We spend many of our waking hours doing work of some kind. If this work isn't satisfying, then it isn't possible for our lives to be satisfying. We can keep this in mind as we continue to make the effort to develop ever-better technology.

WHAT IS
TECHNOLOGY?

Introspection, for most of us, is not something we're taught. As kids, or at least as kids who didn't have screens in front of us constantly, there was plenty of free time, time for doing nothing in particular, that could be spent thinking about how we think, imagining things, and wondering about things. I was one of those kids who spent a lot of time daydreaming. Even in school, I spent more time in school journaling and doodling in notebooks than taking notes.

I was never taught techniques for introspection until I encountered Buddhism in my early twenties. Most of us aren't taught it at all. In early elementary school when my teachers asked me to share how I felt, all I knew how to do was explain what I thought. I didn't know that my feelings arose inside my body or had sensations attached to them. I didn't know that these inward states sang with information about my nature and could tell me whether I was aligned with it or not. I just felt things wildly and muddled through.

My religious education happened in parallel to my secular schooling. My parents made me attend Hebrew school on Tuesday afternoons and Sunday mornings throughout my childhood. It wasn't much help. I didn't detect any wisdom in it until recently; I'm getting to be pretty interested in Judaism these days. I find the Jewish tradition teaches me where I've come from generation by generation. But it wasn't what taught me where I come from moment by moment.

I encountered Buddhism as a college student studying religion and music. Some professors at my school were trained meditators who saw meditation as fundamental to learning as well as to living, and taught it as being every bit as important in a liberal education as the books and works we studied in other classes. So I studied Buddhism historically and philosophically, but I also learned to practice meditation every day, a practice I have kept to this day. When I first started meditating, getting to know my own mind felt like a hopeless task. I had twenty years of cobwebs to clear out. Even now, with a fading memory of college, and a daily meditative practice, I feel as if I'm just learning to walk. When I listen to Buddhist teachers, it's as though I'm looking into a mirror for the first time in my life. When I sit, it's like meeting myself. And on many days, when I get up from sitting, I wonder, "Why haven't I ever met myself before?"

Soon after college, I became a full-time technology reporter, covering daily news for the consumer tech industry. I loved writing and computers and so thought it would be a perfect fit. But I kept finding that rather than imagining a good future and building toward it, the tech companies I covered were lured by irresistible financial incentives to focus on short-term goals. This short-term news cycle created a narrative of endless battle, with companies racing to match each other feature-for-feature and jostling to stomp on the competition. It felt more like sports than technology, with millions of avid fans fighting each other on the sidelines in the comments section. These fans cared as passionately about their home screens as football fans do about their home teams, complete with all the name-calling and trash-talking. After five years, I quit my job and started making music and working for Burning Man, but I kept looking back at the tech companies I'd left behind. Behind the competition and the posturing, there were smart people coming up with innovative and creative ideas that had huge potential to change our daily lives. I was still interested in what had brought me to the digital world in the first place: the question of what we do with technology and how we apply it to our personal lives, our relationships, our jobs, and our societies.

<<<< DEFINING TECHNOLOGY >>>>

The word "technology" is often used as shorthand for computers, smartphones, other Internet-connected devices, and the software we run on them. But that takes these devices out of context, as if they exist separately from other technologies that have come before them or surround them. So for a broader definition of technology, I'll start with the one developed by Kevin Kelly, the founding executive editor of *Wired* magazine. Before *Wired*, Kelly was editor and publisher of the *Whole Earth Catalog*, one of the most cutting-edge, futuristic publications of the late 1960s and early 1970s. He wrote a very good story called *What Technology Wants*.[1] His book describes technology as a realm, far more than a subcategory of human activity. To him, it's more like the seventh kingdom of life, alongside plants, animals, fungi, and the various kinds of microorganisms. Technology does not just provide utility, according to Kelly, it is a growing, breathing connector of all living things.

"Technology is stitching together all the minds of the living, wrapping the planet in a vibrating cloak of electronic nerves," Kelly writes. "[E]ntire continents of machines conversing with one another, the whole aggregation watching itself through a million cameras posted daily. How can this not stir that organ in us that is sensitive to something larger than ourselves?" But the technological realm "is not God; it is too small. It is not utopia. It is not even an entity. It is a becoming that is only beginning."[2]

Kelly traces the word "technology" back to its Greek origins, and the word turns out to be surprisingly rare. It merges two ideas: *techne*—art, skill, cleverness, or ingenuity—and *logos*—words, speech, or literacy. Kelly finds it knit together by Aristotle into *technelogos*, but it's unclear in context what the word means. "Is he concerned with the 'skill of words,' or the 'speech about art' or maybe a literacy of craft?" Kelly asks.[3] Technology wasn't a term used to describe wheels and gears and cranes in ancient Greece.

After Aristotle, the word went dormant for a while, until the Industrial Revolution. By then, its meaning was tangled up with other conceptual inventions, like *art* and *craft* and *culture*, and "technology" was revived to describe the new, now exploding realm of products and processes invented through scientific research, industry, mechanization, and automation.

These unbundled terms don't satisfy Kelly, so he coins a new term, "the technium," to describe that sphere of activity and uses it the way people commonly use "technology" or "technologies" to describe whole systems. To Kelly, the word technology can refer to a *specific* technology, like radar. But he wants a new word to encompass technologies and all their self-amplifying effects.

"The technium extends beyond shiny hardware to include culture, art, social institutions, and intellectual creations of all types," Kelly writes. "It includes intangibles like software, law, and philosophical concepts. And most important, it includes the generative impulses of our inventions to encourage more tool making, more technology invention, and more self-enhancing connections."[4]

This is the scale at which I want to talk about technology. Even when we zoom in on little pieces of technology, such as smartphones or social media, we can't lose sight of the *technium*—the history, the social relations, and the natural and technological ecosystems that support those pieces. Our personal technological choices don't take place in a vacuum.

Most of us are okay with thinking of computers as technology. We're also okay with including cars, microwaves, electric razors, and other things we plug in. What about typewriters? What about books? Are we starting to leave the comfortable category of technology? What about meditation? What about language?

A simple definition covers all of these things:

Technology is the application of knowledge to change our environment.

While that may seem too broad, it's actually rather concrete. Whether it works just once or changes things forever, any method, process, or system we use to change our environment is a technology. The technology is not just the hardware; it's also the software that runs on it. If a program on your phone counts as a technology, then a program in your mind counts, too.

Here are three examples to make it more concrete: the *smartphone, language,* and *religion.*

<<<< SMARTPHONES >>>>

In the early twenty-first century, human beings grew a new appendage. It was quite unlike any other part of the human body, but it bore some similarities. This new appendage also had a new set of organs. It gave human beings new ways to see, hear, sense motion, think, and remember. Most of all, it gave them new ways to talk to each other.

At first, humans called their new appendages "smartphones," because these detachable appendages resembled the cellular telephones humans used to project their voices and talk to one another across long distances. But that resemblance was only superficial. Smartphones were much more deeply connected to the human brain than any previous phones ever were, and their powers extended far beyond the human voice.

Before the telephone, the sensorium of the human body did not extend very far beyond the body at all. Humans could see, hear, and smell things in their immediate vicinity, and they could only feel and taste things that were actually touching them. Only imaginary sense experiences extended further than that. After the radio and the telephone emerged, it became possible to extend some senses using stationary instruments that people placed in their environments, but the people had to stay in place to use them. Some clever inventions amplified basic human senses a few times, like eyeglasses, binoculars, and megaphones, but never far beyond the maximum range of natural human faculties.

Cellular phones changed the way humans behaved. Cell phones extended the sense of hearing and the range of the human voice beyond the horizon. Now people could talk directly to one another as if they were side by side, no matter where either person was. That changed human behavior dramatically, but only through that one sense.

Smartphones (as they were known in the early twenty-first century) changed much more than that. They extended the human mind to planetary dimensions. People didn't even have to hold information inside their own heads anymore; they could store it in their new external appendages, and they could even pull it down from a shared global memory. They could transmit their vision and hearing to anyone else looking or listening anywhere, instantly. They could join in the activities of people anywhere on the globe from right where they were. It was a dramatic evolution in what the human body could do.

The capabilities of these new organs changed the way humans live together. Now they were always connected to each other and their web of messages and ideas. Individuals could know one another's precise location all the time. People regularly checked out of their physical surroundings—including the other people with them—to visit virtual places full of other beings. Some of those beings were the avatars of living people. Others were *artificial beings* living in virtual worlds. After human beings had the mobile Internet, their lives, their habitats, and their evolutionary future would soon barely resemble their earlier forms.

< < < < LANGUAGE > > > >

Language does two basic things: it gives structure to our thoughts, and it allows us to express them. It's not the only way to do either of those things, but it's a very good way. Shortly after humans developed language, pretty much everything changed for us. Most importantly, we could communicate much more clearly with each other. We could plan, we could cooperate on complex tasks, and we could even discuss abstract concepts. This gave us a much more profound sense of what was going on in other people's minds.

Immediately, our economic relationships changed as we became able to collaborate on more interesting things, and our social relationships changed as we developed much more sophisticated ideas about personhood. These transformations happened simultaneously and built on each other. Language changed the world. It changed our inner worlds directly and immediately, enabling us to find new ways to change the outer world through new technologies.

This is the reproductive quality of technology that provoked Kevin Kelly to discuss it like a form of life. "Just as in Darwinian evolution, tiny improvements [in technology] are rewarded with more copies, so that innovations spread steadily through the population. Older ideas merge and hatch idea-lings . . . The technium can really only be understood as a type of evolutionary life."[5] This example also demonstrates what tech people mean when they use the word "platform." Language was a new platform on which we could construct many more technologies and applications. Before we created language, none of the technologies that it enabled were possible.

Swift, the programming language used by Apple for the OS X and iOS operating systems, is clearly a technology. C++, a low-level programming language behind software you use every day, is clearly a technology. We call such programming systems "languages" because they give structure to the programming environment, and they allow programmers to express their programs.

There's nothing inherent in the hardware of a computer that gives rise to C++. The language C++ is a logical invention of humans that takes advantage of the properties of computers for new purposes. That's just what human languages do with the properties of our brains. I'm not saying that brains are computers, minds are programming environments, or that thoughts are programs, only that English, Spanish, Arabic, and Swift are all languages, applications of information that are deployed to communicate and change the environment.

< < < < RELIGION > > > >

One definition of religion is the institution of a shared story to explain the meaning of life. That religious story was imposed as an intermediary between individual people and the world they share, providing them comforting explanations and grounding daily practices. Before literacy, this story was told, sung, acted out, and memorized. A designated person could serve as a priest, someone charged with storing and telling the story on behalf of the other people. Eventually, humans learned to store their religious stories on external media, and that's when things really went viral.

Like any technology, religion is enabled by much lower-level innovations like cooperative group living and shared language. It's a platform for more specific applications that help groups who share a religion get along, like particular social values, morals, customs, and rituals. It's a security system, using conformity to ensure the integrity of the group. Like language, religion is also a platform upon which new technologies can be built.

Religion requires regular maintenance updates and occasional new features. For example, when electric lights were invented, religious rules in Judaism about "lighting fires" on the Sabbath had to be reinterpreted with new technicalities. Sometimes, when there are big social changes, there is a push for a whole religious program to be updated to change with the times.

In short, religion is analogous to software in many ways. If you are not following a religion, you write your own spiritual practice from scratch. With religion, you're given a platform or tool you can use.

The surest sign of a successful technology is any lasting improvement it makes to humans' internal lives. A spiritual practice need not have all the institutional tools that a religion does, but it can still use techniques such as chant, meditation, and story. Whether they reorient us inward or outward, spiritual practices help human beings direct their attention, that essential control mechanism of consciousness, so we don't lose our place in the story of our lives.

Religion and spiritual practice are surely not perfect technologies. We've needed to invent supplementary technologies beyond religion in order to make sense of the world, such as the scientific method and all the improvements to agriculture, medicine, and engineering that it enabled. But religion is one of our oldest, most adaptive technologies. It sprung up everywhere people lived and did what many social media platforms purport to do now: it made the mind larger and the world smaller.

<<<< TECHNOLOGY AS RELATIONSHIP >>>>

Smartphones, language, and spiritual practice are just three examples of how technologies can be understood in different but equally useful ways. We can think of technologies as extensions of our organic selves, enhancing our skills and senses through the application of our knowledge. Or we can think of them as external objects, things we engineer to accomplish specific tasks. We can use whichever of those stories is most useful to us. The point is that it's all technology either way.

Our relationship to computers, or to the social networks we use online, can't be separated from our relationship to language, that fundamental human technology. But computing technology is rather new and poorly understood considering how much we use it. We need to understand how computers are continuous with all the other kinds of technology we use to affect our world. All our technologies extend our innate knowledge and power. The key is to learn to exercise all our technology with the same sense of responsibility, whether it's digital, analog, mental, or physical.

In order to do that, though, we must be careful to understand what technology changes about human life. When the applications of our knowledge change the world around us, we have to adjust. We have to update our internal technologies, our *spiritual* technologies, to adapt to new outside realities. Sometimes technology makes reality easier, offering us convenience and reducing our suffering. But in other cases, it can have challenging consequences. In the United States, for example, the automobile liberated the individual's sense of time and space, freeing us to roam the Earth under our own power. But in our haste to enjoy that freedom, we built a suburban lifestyle around the car that distanced us from our communities and isolated us in our homes. Our country is starting to recognize the crises this lifestyle has caused, and to offer solutions to them, but it has taken decades to reach this point. The advent of smartphones and social media is much more recent, and we haven't had time to adjust to their consequences.

Our use of high technology can fragment our attention, trigger our insecurities and traumas, interfere with our relationships, and violate our privacy. But these consequences are not problems with "technology." They're the side effects of some technologies, and they can be remedied in turn with other technologies. We have mindfulness technologies to train our minds and hearts to concentrate on the good. We have community technologies that can promote inclusivity and authenticity. Spiritual practice is *technology*, and it's vital in adapting our lives to the digital age.

TECHNOLOGY AND SPIRITUALITY

It's tempting to think of the Internet as a place. We've learned to relate to it as a world on the other side of a window. We open the window, see this virtual world on the other side, and we can just barely reach through using these strange controls we've learned to manipulate. We can't enter with our whole bodies and walk around the place—not yet, anyway—but in order to access the Internet, we do have to go there. When we turn our attention back to the physical world, we leave the Internet. It makes sense that the Internet feels like a place. That's how we've designed it.

Even though we can just barely reach into this apparent world with the surface of our fingertips or the sounds of our voices, software companies have built features on the Internet that give it one of the most important qualities of our frequently inhabited places: other people. Even if we were skeptical of the Internet's placeness at first glance, it's impossible not to be drawn in when we see other people moving around in there, talking, and taking pictures. This sensation makes it easy for us to imagine the Internet as some kind of game full of other players, with rules much simpler than those of everyday life. (And for millions of players of massive multiplayer games, it is exactly like that.)

But clearly the Internet placeness is a metaphor. It may feel like everyone in a comment thread—or even in a virtual dungeon full of goblins—is in the same place together, but it's not true. The others probably left their message an hour ago and are back to work by now. Even if anyone else is present at the same time, it's not as though they're in a room with you. They're looking at a different instance of the same data rendered somewhere else. You're communicating through a long, byzantine contraption from two different places.

But that doesn't make your shared experience any less real. You're both having experiences as real as any other. But the experience isn't taking place in the Internet. It's taking place in your body as you interact with the information on the screen. A real place provides an embodied experience. Even if you were in a three-dimensional virtual reality environment projected into a helmet, you'd still be in the same *place* as you would be if the power went out and the helmet blinked off.

But if the power went out, you would lose contact with the people you were speaking to online. Something about your environment would have changed. A human connection would be severed. That's as real as anything. But where did it go?

This kind of weirdness is what makes the newly networked world feel unfamiliar. That alienness increases the temptation to treat online conversations or experiences as taking place in their own discrete, virtual space. The rules aren't the same there as here. Surely that must be somewhere else.

But we're tricking ourselves by believing that. The Internet doesn't actually have the qualities to make it a place. That illusion of "going there" and "coming back" is caused by inadequate technology. We don't actually leave the conversations we have online when we shut off our screen. We pause our connection to them, but they're still there.

The mobile revolution demonstrates this clearly. Now that we have battery-powered, wireless computers, more and more messages get pushed to us when they are sent instead of just waiting for us to check them. And when our phones receive them, they buzz in our pockets, and we feel them. With our real, embodied legs! Some friend of ours reached through the window to the Internet and tapped us on the leg. There's no virtual reality in the middle. It's all reality, the same one we're in all the time.

<<<< BEING PRESENT EVERYWHERE AT ONCE >>>>

Much of the popular writing about what tech is doing to us posits two different realities: a physical one and a digital or virtual one. But Nathan Jurgenson, a brilliant theorist, coined a much-needed term for this distinction as a fallacy. He calls it "digital dualism," and to me it's the same kind of metaphysical misconception that the Buddha warns about. The separate self, separation in general—that's all an illusion. It does us no good to draw borders here. It doesn't bring us deeper into "the real." It isolates us further.

"For many," Jurgenson writes, "maintaining the fiction of the collective loss of the offline for everyone else is merely an attempt to construct their own personal time-outs as more special, as allowing them to rise above those social forces of distraction that have ensnared the masses. 'I am real. I am the thoughtful human. You are the automaton.'"[1]

The excerpt is from Jurgenson's 2012 essay, "The IRL Fetish," one of my favorite writings about technology. "IRL" is Internet jargon for "in real life." It's used in context like this: "I'm a Level 40 Paladin! But I'm a stock-broker IRL." I chose in real life for the title of this book to make the point that real life is all there is. There's no escape. If you spend hours of your day being a Level 40 Paladin slaying wild beasts with your broadsword, that's part of who you are, and so are the consequences. Here's more from Jurgenson on that.

> Facebook doesn't curtail the offline but depends on it. What is most crucial to our time spent logged on is what happened when logged off; it is the fuel that runs the engine of social media. The photos posted, the opinions expressed, the check-ins that fill our streams are often anchored by what happens when disconnected and logged-off. The Web has everything to do with reality; it comprises real people with real bodies, histories, and politics. It is the fetish objects of the offline and the disconnected that are not real.[2]

This totally comprises my stance on digital dualism. Treating the web as though it isn't real, or as if it's an alternate reality, ignores the consequences it has for us right here in this reality, the *only* reality. If we aren't mindful of the fact that our *real selves* are online, interacting with other *real selves*, we're vulnerable to the same pitfalls of distraction and alienation that get us when we forget to be mindful in the offline parts of our lives.

But the unity of digital and analog reality doesn't mean that the subjective *experiences* of one or the other aren't radically different. We've only had digital experiences for a minutely small fraction of the human experience. Our way of being in the world evolved in response to an analog environment. We still live in that reality, but the rules of it have changed suddenly. We've extended it and layered new kinds of experiences on top of it. When our friend taps us on the leg through our phone, she makes physical contact with the real you. But she doesn't feel your leg; she feels cold glass. You don't feel the tap of her fingers; you feel a sharp, mechanical buzz.

The early notion of virtual reality from science fiction is that humans could be like gods, creating worlds where our own made-up rules applied. But the future we got is even stranger than that. We're still the same fragile, embodied beings we used to be, but now we have a layer on top of our environment where people and computers can interact at a distance.

Our precise real-world position is usually knowable to others. We can share what we're seeing and hearing to anyone in real time. We can have a conversation with anyone anywhere in the world, and we can do it in complete silence. It's not that we're learning how to invent new places. It's that we're learning how to be everywhere at once. "Wherever you go, there you are," Jon Kabat-Zinn said in his great book on mindfulness.[3] But it's hard enough to be present in one place. We haven't even begun to learn how to be present everywhere at once.

There's a crucial lesson here that is both obvious and easy to forget: Those are real people you're talking to online! When avatars are arguing on the Internet, there are real human bodies controlling them, breathing hard, clenching their jaws, typing too fast, groaning in frustration! If you could see their body language, you'd probably worry about them. But in the most common kinds of online interactions, you can't. They're just a smiling face and a name—or a cartoon of an octopus and a made-up nickname—and you just have to imagine their tone of voice.

This is what makes it hard to design social software. Computers were such blunt instruments when people first started using them to interact at a distance, and they've only gotten slightly better. Even touch-controlled computers are cold and hard and inflexible. We've reached the point where clear and realistic video conversations can be held wirelessly on most computers, but they don't feel nearly as natural as walking side by side with someone. Video calls are a beautiful, miraculous technology, but there's a reason we don't have most of our face-to-face conversations staring at each other head-on without moving.

Real-time calls with video or voice are possible all the time now, but we have them infrequently relative to less involved kinds of online interactions. We've realized for a variety of social and technical reasons that we can pack much more human contact into a day if we break most of it down into small written or photographed chunks that can be sent and received at any time. Most of our online conversation is a new kind of conversation, one that only requires the presence of the participants for moments long enough to enter a response. They don't even have to read the previous comments. There's no listening required. It's a model of conversation designed for convenience, but the trade-off is that it's not designed for empathy.

Thich Nhat Hanh says that understanding is the foundation of love. Unless you can understand, and thus empathize, with another person, you can't actually love them, you can only love the idea of them. The practice of deep listening, which involves mindful listening without judgment or interruption, is almost impossible in online interactions.

Now that the whole world can share one public

sphere, groups who can't tolerate each other are forced into unpleasant interaction, and everyone else has to watch. This has much worse consequences the less empowered one is by society. The popular feminist website Jezebel, for example, gets mobbed by dozens or hundreds of abusive, violent, male-or-anonymous trolls sharing images of women being raped and decapitated every day. As Amanda Hess wrote in Pacific Standard earlier this year, "Of the 3,787 people who reported harassing incidents [online] from 2000 to 2012 to the volunteer organization Working to Halt Online Abuse, 72.5 percent were female."[4]

A 2012 study from the George Mason University Center for Climate Change Communication and some other institutions found that angry blog comments cause people to entrench in their existing beliefs instead of listening to one another and learning something.[5] And the companies who create the venues for this have little incentive to do anything about it. According to their bottom lines, both the mob behavior and the outrage that rightly accompanies it are a win-win. More grist for the content mill.

The motivations of the companies developing the software most people use for online conversation are conflicted. They have the high-minded motivation to create something that feels like a good way to have a conversation, because if they don't, people won't use it. But most of them are supported by advertising, so they also have to build something that will be used in repetitive ways for lots of time, where it won't feel weird if the software injects a little precisely targeted marketing from time to time. These two motivations can't always be reconciled, and which one a company favors will vary by how healthy its bottom line is.

Luckily for us, it's not up to those companies how we use this software, just like it's not up to the designers and engineers of our sidewalks and lobbies and restaurants how we interact in those spaces. There are constraints in every environment on how we can behave, but it's up to us to thrive within those constraints. Yes, environments contribute to our mood, and the bounds of acceptable behavior are ultimately set in law, but the vast majority of our human contact takes place in the gray area where how we present ourselves and treat each other is up to us. This is true online and offline, and our responsibility to each other is the same.

Unfortunately, it's harder to behave well in online interactions. Communication technologies are maturing fast, but they're still barely scratching the surface of what made human interaction interesting to us for our entire evolutionary history.

The delayed, text-based conversations that make

up most of our online interactions have no facial expressions, body language, or tone of voice. Those are crucial sources of meaning. They can sometimes be enough to clearly understand someone who's speaking in a different language! Emoticons and bold or italicized text are pretty poor substitutes. Even in the smaller number of online conversations we have face-to-face or voice-to-voice using video chat, there's no physical contact, and the rules about eye contact are all thrown off. Where do you look: At the other person's eyes? At the camera, so they see your eyes? At your *own* eyes in the little window on the side? This is not a medium that feels comfortable for human conversation yet.

The social context of conversations is also different. Human conversation evolved as a largely ephemeral art. The words in front of you and in short-term memory were the rails on which the conversation rode. We couldn't search through the history and dig up every little contradiction or misstep. Only the most profound statements, whether beautiful or painful, were durable enough to remain in memory. If people were going through the effort to transcribe a conversation, it had to be of serious importance. Maybe we took greater risks in our speech because we knew our words couldn't be used against us as easily. Then again, maybe we were less concerned with facts and accuracy.

Regardless, much of our conversation now takes place in an indelible, searchable record. If you say something publicly that contradicts something you said a long time ago, chances are good that someone will find it and use it against you. People will split hairs over your exact wording, preserved for all to see, instead of trusting your intent and letting your words wash over them. And though some online conversation tools give you the ability to retract what you say, that can make things worse, especially if someone took a screenshot. These constraints make conversations feel more mechanical and serious. It's intense to discuss things in text. It requires mindfulness to avoid mistakes and maintain right speech.

Right speech is an old problem with spiritual consequences. The Buddha spoke about it in the Sutta Nipata: "The person abiding by a certain dogmatic view, considering it is the highest in the world, claims 'This is the most excellent,' and disparages other views different from that as inferior. As a result, he is not free from disputation." This is a great risk when the mode of conversation privileges the digital record over the face-to-face encounter with another being. It's an essential part of the Buddha's path to avoid this. "A disciplined man does not engender dogmatic views in the world either by knowledge or by rule or rite. Therefore, he does not consider himself 'superior,' 'inferior,' or 'equal'. . . .

By overcoming all the theories based on seen, heard or thought he is a sage who has released his burden and is liberated."[6] How did the Buddha, thousands of years ago, know so much about how to fix online conversations? It's not just because he was the Buddha. It's because the spiritual pitfalls of all human conversations are essentially the same.

There are some good things about the online mode of communication, though. Time-delayed conversations do reduce the sense of the other person's presence, but they also allow responses to be thought through and measured out before sending. Online conversations also provide us wonderful powers of reference that we don't have in person. We can easily drop in links alongside our conversations to vast resources of related information, diagrams, images, and videos.

Ephemerality can be useful for some kinds of conversations—and tech companies have taken advantage of this with services like Snapchat, which offers an illusion of impermanence by making messages disappear from users' phones. But even though Snapchat deletes messages from its servers, any recipient could easily copy them or take a screenshot to preserve them. But there is also a good reason for archives and record keeping, both on the personal level—to maintain records of love letters, thoughts, and friendships—and also on the historical level—

as people look back at successful strategies for online organizing, for holding public figures accountable for their comments (remember Anthony Weiner? Donald Sterling?), and for capturing and sharing inspirational moments around the world, from Tiananmen Square and Zuccotti Park to the Arab Spring.

There is plenty of space for both off- and online conversations. The question is whether a given conversation is best held online or in person. As I write, for example, I'm in the midst of a difficult, slow-moving negotiation with my seven-member house. That's a lot of busy people to wrangle together for face-to-face meetings, especially when they're long and drawn out and exhausting. The momentum would fail if we weren't using email to keep things on the rails, supporting our in-person conversations. New technology is helping us work out our problems in ways that were impossible before.

But all these ways to converse require different social skills, many of which are brand new to the species. When the same conversation inevitably jumps from in-person to text message to email, it's hard to adjust to the new environment on the fly, especially when the topic is difficult. When you're stressed out at work and decide to relieve the pressure by checking your social networks, only to see someone has posted an article that offends and enrages you, it's easy to take your stress out on that person and call them an idiot or a racist when you don't have to do so to their face. It's easier to slip out of a mindful posture without the in-person reminders we've evolved to expect. Offline social graces are hard enough, but online manners are even harder to control.

One major problem is that it's hard to remain present in the body during an online conversation. When we don't feel people's eyes on us, we might be less mindful of how we're carrying our body, and we might be curled up and defensive or tense and shaky without realizing it. We're concentrating harder on the message, on the virtual thing that we're sending, so we're paying less attention to the feelings behind it. Those feelings are what give rise to our words and actions, but without mindfulness of the feelings, our reactions to them are out of control. Our own feelings are hard enough to watch when we're riled up in conversation. It's all the more difficult to be mindful of the embodied feelings of the person on the receiving end of our words, about whom we have barely any clues.

It's easy for able-bodied and neurotypical people to take conversation skills for granted. Learning them is just part of growing up. It's easy not to think about how much harder conversation is for someone who is blind or deaf, or who is developmentally less able to read social cues from facial expressions. People with those obstacles struggle to adjust and keep up with what can seem like impossible social demands.

The constraints of online communication can suddenly put otherwise able-bodied and able-minded people into a comparable situation, only they aren't used to struggling to hold a conversation, so it frequently goes awry. Internet fights go on and on, continuing long after anyone's getting anything valuable from them. People just can't empathize as easily with people who aren't—or at least don't appear to be—right in front of them. I'm sure that will change over generations, but we have to help that process along right now. We have to teach and practice mindfulness as a prerequisite for all encounters online and off. Our relationships depend on it.

Perhaps we should use visualization exercises to help with our online empathy. Before we hit send, we could check in with our body and make sure we feel good about what we're about to say. Then we can imagine the recipient on the other end of the line, sitting at the screen on their desk or scrolling on their phone with their thumb, the excitement in their eye as they're notified of the new message, the emotion on their lips as they read the response. No matter what kind of conversation we're in, we can always remember there's a human being just as fragile and complicated as ourselves on the other side.

MAGIC AND MAYHEM

Imagine you're sitting on a hill at dusk with two friends. The darkness and quiet up here is a rare relief from your buzzing, big-city neighborhoods. The bugs are coming out, now that the air is cooling. You're laughing and telling stories and remembering things you've done together. In the lulls of silence, you gaze up at the darkening sky. One friend sees a bright point of light overhead, one of the first stars to come out. "What star is that?" she asks. You draw your phone from your pocket, unlock it, and tap the dark blue icon emblazoned with the Big Dipper. You raise your phone to the sky, and the answer appears to you. "That's not a star," you say with interest. "That's Venus!"

Your favorite singer in the world posts a clip from a new video. A song you know and love begins to play, but now it's the soundtrack to a new story. In the video, she's sitting at a small table in a funky, old diner, staring out the window with tired eyes, singing the first verse. Wait a second. You recognize that place. You compose a message: "Is that Loui's in Providence, Rhode Island? I've had breakfast at that table before!" A minute later, your favorite singer in the world responds directly to you: "It sure is. Spent some weird mornings there."

In San Francisco, one third of food stamp recipients are unnecessarily cut from benefits. A new app called Promptly can send text notifications to let families know if they're in danger of being cut. Apps aren't just for anecdotes. There are apps to keep families fed and help them save money, to speed up the response times of emergency services, and to help public health professionals contain epidemics. The number of examples of world-changing civic software will only continue to grow.

New technology can amaze us that way constantly,

simply by working as intended. That's why magic is such a good word for marketing technology. There is a kind of magic in connecting so readily with others, and in having quick and easy access to what we need or want. I want to examine how that relates to a different sense of magic, the palpable quality of a spiritual life. When we're mindful of the causes and conditions surrounding us, something surprising happens. It's not always good. Sometimes it's spectacularly bad. When we're half-present (especially if we're on our phone or checking our email) we miss the awesome in the ordinary.

The stories above demonstrate the kind of magic technology companies want to sell us. If we're fully alive to what feels magical about those moments, it's clear that the technology is just an accessory to the magic, part of the scenery. Smartphones and Internet services aren't characters in the stories, they're just props. The actual sources of the magic in the stories are the connections between human beings. Technology facilitated those connections, but it didn't add its own magic. There's just as much magic of the same kind in stories like the following, no phones required:

It's tense. You're interviewing for a job that's so perfect for you, you can hardly believe it exists. But it makes you nervous. What if they don't

think you're qualified? What if your cover letter was too conversational? What if your outfit
isn't formal enough? What if, what if, what
if? The hiring manager is asking you a question. It involves a long, complicated scenario,
the kind of thing you'd have to deal with every
day. He's intimidating you. But as you listen to
the details, the story begins to sound familiar.
It sounds just like a situation you handled at
your last job. The whole thing replays itself in
your mind as he asks you, "Do you know what
you'd do in that situation?" Everyone around
the table looks at you. "Yes," you say, with light
in your eyes, and you watch their faces change
as you tell your story.

On your usual route, you see a man who looks
homeless begging for change. He's on a busy
corner. Dozens of people pass him every minute, but you only see a couple of people drop
coins into his cup. This situation makes you
nervous sometimes. It's hard to determine the
right thing to do. Sometimes, even though it
feels awful, you just walk right past. But now,
as you approach, your eyes meet his. "Can you
spare any change?" he asks you, looking right

at you. You can read so many stories on his face, and you see yourself in the story now that you're before him. "Sure," you find yourself saying. "What's your name?"

Your heart is broken. You can't believe this person you trusted could do something so hurtful to you. It's enough to make you want to give up on people. Just people, in general. They aren't worth the effort. But just as this thought crosses your mind, your roommate comes in the front door. He's been at work all day, and he looks as exhausted as always. You're a little embarrassed to be seen like this. But he puts down his bag and his coat and comes right over to you. He asks you what's wrong. You tell him. He lets you say everything your heart wants to say. He can hear you slowly healing.

Those three stories aren't about "technology" in the way we're used to thinking about it. They don't involve phones or apps or the Internet. They're just expressions of the human spirit, of people affecting one another. To me, this magic is just our ability to connect with each other and the world and the people around us.

The fact that we can connect with other human

beings is miraculous. But to do it, we had to invent technologies like language and culture and literacy and money. We humans have a continuous legacy of building inventions for bringing the faraway up close and making the unknown known to us. That can be good magic.

But magic can be dangerous. Magic can trick people. Magic can upset balances and destroy delicate creations. Technology is amoral. It does its best to follow our guidance. And if we don't guide it well, our magic can blow up in our faces. So if we want to do good in the world, it's important that we practice good magic. Changing the world is not just a matter of knowing how to use one's tools. A person "might perform actions methodically and properly," Chögyam Trungpa Rinpoche taught, "but without knowledge, without the sword that cuts through doubt and hesitation, his action is not really transcendental at all."[1] Without mindfulness behind it, technology is a volatile weapon. To use it carefully takes training and practice.

<<<< EVOLUTION AND PROBLEM-SOLVING >>>>

When I was twenty years old, I had the amazing opportunity to take a wilderness trip to South Africa with my grandmother and all her descendants. While on safari one day, we learned about an evolutionary arms race that inspired an interesting train of thought. There's a cuckoo out there in the bush that is a brood parasite. It lays its eggs in other birds' nests, and the other birds will feed the young cuckoos along with their own. This gives the cuckoos a competitive edge, obviously. So these competitors evolved colored markings on the inside of their throats, so they could tell who was family and who was cuckoo. This worked for a while until the cuckoos managed to evolve these markings for themselves. The race goes on.

These evolutionary responses struck me as quite clever. I anthropomorphized them at first and thought them to be quite human responses, but then I just admitted that they resembled creative and intelligent responses. They exhibited disguise, deception, and cunning, which are seemingly cognitive functions. But these responses evolved over many generations of evolutionary trial and error, not by conscious choice.

This got me thinking about consciousness and its function. It seemed to me that the typical function of consciousness was to make creative choices in rational self-interest, comparable in cleverness to these gradual evolutions. It was the same trial-and-error process of learning from experience, only within the bounds of one organism's lifetime. It was as though consciousness enabled humans to wield evolutionary power on a moment-by-moment basis instead of being limited to the sluggish pace of natural selection.

We could, if we thought carefully about it, create a foolproof disguise like the cuckoo did, but we could do it much more quickly, within the lifetime of one organism, within one day! If a brilliant scientist observed a nest invaded by a cuckoo for a while, saw that the cuckoo baby wasn't getting fed, and noticed the markings in the other baby birds' throats, she could theoretically abduct the cuckoo baby for an hour or two, perform careful plastic surgery to put those markings in its throat, and trick the brood mother into feeding it. Human consciousness and creativity would collapse many generations of haphazard, accidental trial and error into a day's work for one clever organism. So the evolutionary significance of consciousness is dramatic.

The ability to make a choice is an evolutionary power, then. It occurred to me that life forms developed this power in increasingly profound ways over all of evolution. One profound development was fear, a primal characteristic of animal life. The fear response enables a clear evolutionary choice to be made. The fish that swims away goes on to evolve, the one that doesn't gets eaten. But this basic decision merely nudges the evolutionary process. Creative consciousness seems much more powerful. It's instantaneous evolution. It creates knowledge, an invaluable evolutionary cache that improves an individual's fitness and can be transmitted to the next generation. Let's call this ability intelligence.

But using intelligence, we can see that this is still just an evolutionary stepping stone. For one thing, the human mind, our store of knowledge, is a leaky system. It forgets, it makes mistakes, it gets tired, and crucially, it's almost entirely destroyed when an individual dies. Only that which can be taught or externally recorded and recalled by others can survive, and that's a pretty low percentage of the contents of an individual's knowledge.

More importantly, conscious creativity yields fragile solutions. Evolutionary selection may have taken ten thousand tries to nail the cuckoo's ingenious disguise, but after getting it right, that pattern of throat markings is hardwired into the cuckoo genome. Now it happens automatically every time. Sure, conscious humans could come up with that disguise right away, but we'd have to make a new one for each baby, and if we messed up or forgot, the baby is done for.

So, in my twenty-year-old mind, I tried to conceive of an intelligence far more powerful than ours, one that is truly equivalent to the power of evolution, with the power to alter its organism's own genome! This is a little ridiculous to think about, at least in Earth terms. The energy intensiveness of the intelligence capable of this, let alone the actual process of gene alteration, would surely be absurd. But one can conceive of an environment where the evolution of this intelligence is possible. Imagine those aliens!

Even though we often draw a distinction between "natural" and "technological" domains, there's something intriguingly similar about the processes that drive both of them. Biological evolution and technological progress are both about problem solving. They're both about making it easier for life to survive and thrive. They're both driven by experimentation and learning from failure. And they both make the impossible possible. It's no mystery why: Intelligence, the faculty that enables technology, is a product of evolution, too. It's all the same process of refining life on Earth.

Both evolution and technology are more impressive when considered at various scales. One cuckoo sneaking its egg into one nest might seem merely clever, even cruel. But what about the species it attacks evolving secret markings inside its throat to break through the disguise? And the cuckoo eventually adapting them, too? Even in the brutality of this example, a beauty emerges over time. An epic struggle for survival. And as the solutions begin to seem more ingenious and unlikely, they become awe-inspiring. Science fiction writer Arthur C. Clarke said, "Any sufficiently advanced technology is indistinguishable from magic."[2] I'd say the same for any sufficiently advanced biology, because it's simply magical that life can solve its own problems.

Touch screens. Voice control. Video chat. These are everyday kinds of interactions we have now, but they're also like the magic powers people have written stories about for all of history. Crystal balls. Spoken spells. Astral projection. Maybe touch screens seem less magical than crystal balls to us, since we use them every day. But I imagine that a wireless, Internet-connected tablet would pass as a scrying mirror to any early-modern period person. Judging by our current civilization's fascination with black slabs of glass, it seems like the magic is not all gone.

At the beginning of the film *2001: A Space Odyssey*, the sudden appearance of a geometrically perfect black monolith drives the early humans into a frenzy that culminates in the invention of the murder weapon, one of the oldest human technologies. When the monolith returns in 2001, it calls the space-age humans to the outer solar system. In the real world, the monolith didn't reach the market until 2007, but '01 wasn't a bad guess. As a former tech journalist, the comparison of the iPhone to the *2001* monolith is getting old, but it's still tempting. It's not simply because they're both black rectangles. It's because frenzied reaction to both black rectangles is inspired by the human discovery—and continual rediscovery—of the magic of technology.

Technology companies are selling magic. They use the word earnestly. When talking to insiders, though, tech product people like to speak in terms of solving problems. Nothing really feels like magic unless it improves our lives, relieving a "pain point," to use a common techie term. A good consumer technology should solve "everyday problems" for "everyday people," such as getting government benefits, finding a doctor or affordable healthcare, helping people get on the right bus, or reach the right person. That everyday need is the origin of all technology, after all. From that follows a sort of faith that all one needs to change the world through technology is an understanding of a juicy "everyday problem." Silicon Valley operates under the assumption that financial success, fame, and glory will necessarily follow from that.

In the best case, the consumer tech industry solves a real problem, but it does so in a way that favors profits over durable solutions. When Facebook opened to the public, it created a better way of communicating and maintaining relationships for over a billion people and counting. But its founders realized that, at that scale, their priority should be gathering and selling data about the global population, mainly for advertising purposes. They only had to be the best *available* communication tool to achieve that purpose, not the best *possible*, and their chosen business model actually works *against* the goal of being the best possible way to communicate in many subtle ways, which we'll see later.

And in the worst case, the "everyday problem" mentality in Silicon Valley produces results that are just frivolous and grossly wasteful. As soon as solving an "everyday problem" became the only elevator pitch venture capitalists would listen to, overwhelmingly white and male start-up founders just racked their brains for everyday problems they shared with wealthy, overwhelmingly white and male VCs. Countless millions of dollars are willingly set on fire, given to freshly minted computer science majors who have written the fifth clone of an already successful app like Instagram, because an "everyday problem" for young, rich people is that their $600 smartphone isn't useful enough without an even better way to put a nostalgic filter on this morning's photo of a $6 latte.

The tech industry is insular enough that if the right person wants his or her own problem solved, he or she can mobilize lots of money and resources to solve it, even if it's not a problem that the rest of the world has. This can result in what looks from the outside to be extravagant waste, while everybody on the inside is working hard and getting rich.

There are countless pressing problems the tech

industry is in the best position of anyone to solve. The most obvious is truly global access to the digital economy instead of concentrating on already wealthy nations. These companies are also experts in electricity consumption; extracting, using, and reusing natural resources, traffic and weather data all around the world; and other planet-threatening logistical challenges. Sure, some of them are making improvements in these fields, but the mix could be so much better.

Most social problems just aren't on the radar of the kinds of people at the helm of the dominant tech companies. As Jaron Lanier writes in *You Are Not a Gadget*, "I fear that we are beginning to design ourselves to suit digital models of us, and I worry about a leaching of empathy and humanity in that process."[5]

The focuses of the dominant companies in the so-called "Attention Economy" also cloud their judgment about what habits of communication and connectivity are healthy for the individual. For companies supported by advertising or continuous purchasing of new and shiny things, calm, satisfied, mindful people are not exactly ideal customers.

Paraphrasing Beat poet Allen Ginsberg, an early Facebook engineer named Jeff Hammerbacher told *Bloomberg Businessweek* in 2011, "The best minds of my generation are thinking about how to make people click ads."[3]

Ginsberg himself might have written a eulogy for humanity of biblical proportions about this situation. Hammerbacher, in more matter-of-fact, Silicon Valley fashion, added, "That sucks."[4]

<<<< THE AMPLIFIER >>>>

Technology isn't dangerous by itself, but it has a risky property. The danger of technology is what it amplifies in our own nature. We've amplified human civilization to this planetary size that's too loud, too bright, and too hot for us to handle. We haven't had time to grow into our new shoes yet.

Now that we've got global mass media, it's possible to compare notes on what people want the future to look like. People all over the world seem to want some form of broader and deeper interconnectedness with each other. Communication looks like an emerging global value. The circulation of money and trade is a kind of communication we've been building for millennia. Now the unstoppable growth of the Internet is accelerating global communication to the speed of thought. Humankind seems hell-bent on magnifying itself to planetary scale.

If you imagine an interconnected, global human mind as the adulthood of our species, we're still babies. The only things we can do as a coordinated planet are eat, poop, and throw tantrums. On the individual human scale, we can handle babies. Yes, we have to spend a lot of energy taking care of them, and we worry about them constantly. But even though we can't protect them from everything, at least we can protect them from themselves. They'd be helpless without adults. But now look at us all together, the infant human species. We have no grown-ups to protect us. If we hurt ourselves, no one can kiss us and make it feel better.

Fundamentally, our nature has not changed much throughout all of history, though our lifestyles and habits have changed dramatically many times. But the universal challenges of human life are still the same. We're still mortal, but we often feel immortal. We're still totally interconnected with all things, but we often feel separate. We're still a tiny part of the grand story of the cosmos, but we often feel like the center of the action. We all search for connection and meaning in life, but constant turbulence and change makes it hard to hold onto anything.

All wisdom traditions basically teach that the problems of human life arise from these misunderstandings of our nature. So as long as we amplify a misunderstanding of ourselves, we amplify those problems, just as we have already done to a global scale. The wisdom traditions have also proposed practices such as meditation to solve that misunderstanding. Those practices are still right here waiting for us to implement them.

Our species may have this glorious potential for interconnectedness, but for now, we're still individuals. We each have our own skills and knowledge. Technology is how we apply our skills and knowledge in the world, so it amplifies what's inside us. It widens the circle of our effects. It amplifies the effects of what we know, but acting from what we know also reflects what we don't know. Our technology is only as good a solution to our problems as our knowledge will allow. If we don't know everything about the problem, our solution will almost always have unforeseen consequences. The amplifier of technology may be necessary to help us all reach each other someday and become an adult species. But that will only work if the individual natures that we're amplifying are ready for that. And judging by the way things are going on Earth, we are not ready yet.

The early stages of global communication have tested our readiness in many ways, and we can already see results. There have been waves of unprecedented transparency, where powerful institutions like governments and corporations could no longer keep their secrets from the world. The communication age enabled leaks and revelations, since the acts of a few intrepid people—heroic and nefarious ones alike—could be amplified so quickly and widely.

The leaks by U.S. intelligence contractor Edward Snowden forced American society to confront some of its most cynical and unwholesome tendencies. Other leaks, like the massive caches of diplomatic cables released by Wikileaks, had more chaotic effects, some important and good, others reckless and destabilizing. Meanwhile, the same technological forces are amplifying the empowered interests' hunger for control, enabling them to build mechanisms of surveillance and control over once-private realms of life. It's an information arms race, and it's no less futile than any other. "The haystacks are enormous," the sci-fi author and journalist Cory Doctorow says, "but they still have the same number of needles in them."[6]

The same pattern can be seen reflected in culture. Intolerance and discrimination are amplified by the new media, emboldening and unifying the isolated people who harbor those feelings, perhaps inspiring them to act more boldly out of those hateful, fearful places in their hearts. Everyday expressions of racist hatred, while present everywhere, used to be localized. But now, when a hashtag like #hitlerwasright starts trending, the whole world can see it and must feel its sting.

The other side of that effect is that these painful messages more quickly reach the ears of the moderate, tolerant majority. Some of those people in the center may have placidly believed that extreme intolerance on the fringes was not a pressing problem, but the amplifier of technology makes it loud and clear to them. Now cultural darkness can't be ignored and must be confronted. Sexism, racism, and all dimensions of xenophobia have gained a global stage on the Internet. But attention—the bright light of day—guided by the amplified voices of people with integrity and courage, may be the only way to dry up that swamp of human problems.

Technology amplifies human nature in all directions. It makes small-scale problems into large-scale problems, but it also does the opposite. Social media is rich with examples of this because it gives to individuals many powers that were formerly only available to elite institutions. People are still uneasy about it, unsure of how to handle it. That's why the media story about it swings so wildly between "social media is liberating humankind from bondage" and "social media is melting our neurons," back and forth. I think we understand one half of the problem with social media better than the other, and that's the cause of confusion.

It's easier to understand the idea that small power gets dangerous when it's made big. We're all familiar enough with the wants and drives and many kinds of craziness that individual humans have because we have them too. We look at social media, and we see people's selfishness, insecurity, vanity, and greed blown up to public proportions, and that's disgusting. Even when people choose to amplify their positive qualities, the public spectacle seems to change the meaning of those qualities. It makes them seem more self-serving. "Look at me! Notice how good I am!"

This shift of scale seems inappropriate, and it messes with our senses of virtue. Jewish tradition teaches that the highest form of charity is anonymous, because that puts all the attention on the good that was done, not the individual who did it. The ego has self-serving, ulterior motives for doing good, and that can complicate the goodness of a deed. "Ego is always trying to achieve spirituality," Chögyam Trungpa Rinpoche taught. "It is rather like wanting to witness your own funeral."[7] That is, the ego wants to know it is good by being validated once and for all by others, but that will never happen. When we're mindful, we know it will never happen, but we still have to try to be good anyway, without validation. When we see these cries for validation from others online, we can sometimes awaken a little to the futility of this struggle. One of the aims of meditation practice is to learn to see through this voice of ego crying out to be noticed, let it go quiet, and redirect our attention to doing good for its own sake.

Social media can direct vastly more attention at the doer of a deed, so actions performed there can serve the ego. But this is merely a new manifestation of an old problem. It's a bug in how human society evolved to work. The power of the individual messes up the group dynamic when it interferes too much with the power of the collective. We're used to dealing with this problem; it's just worse now that everyone has a planet-sized megaphone. But there's a corresponding amplifying effect of global communication technology in the other direction that we don't understand nearly as well. Between the dawn of civilization and now, we got used to institutionalizing the power of the collective. To direct the group, we made institutions, super-individuals. We built governments and companies and armies and teams that had their own needs, but which were designed to handle group power, unlike our individual minds. Now, for the first time, global communication technology is putting group power in individual hands, and that poses brand-new problems.

This is the power of virality. An example: A young, mild-mannered Vietnamese programmer named Dong Nguyen made a silly smartphone game called *Flappy Bird* in a couple days' work. It was noteworthy for being infuriatingly difficult to play. That novelty touched just the right nerve. Almost overnight, he was overwhelmed by global media attention, and his game began grossing

$50,000 a day. Good for him, everybody thought, but the attention was so searingly intense that he decided to yank the game out of the store and wait for everyone to go away. "I'm sorry 'Flappy Bird' users," Nguyen wrote on Twitter, "twenty-two hours from now, I will take 'Flappy Bird' down. I cannot take this anymore." And so he did. Later, in an interview with *Forbes*, Nguyen explained his decision more thoroughly. "*Flappy Bird* was designed to play in a few minutes when you are relaxed. But it happened to become an addictive product. I think it has become a problem. To solve that problem, it's best to take down *Flappy Bird*. It's gone forever."[8]

In 2012, a video appeared on a popular web forum of American middle school students being viciously mean to their school bus monitor, Karen Klein. The thread became popular because users of the forum were horrified at the abuse these kids were inflicting on this woman. A member of the forum created a $5,000 crowd-funding campaign to send her on a vacation as a nice gesture. The campaign ended up raising more than $700,000. That's 14,000 percent of its funding goal. Some vacation. Klein retired from her job. She donated $100,000 to establish the Karen Klein Anti-Bullying Foundation and kept the rest.[9]

Neither of these people expected such power. They didn't even seek it, but they got it anyway. To come to terms with both the immediacy and potential of global communication, we need to take the time and make the effort to understand ourselves, our motivations and intentions, before amplifying anything online. The problem is not the "share" button itself but how often and carelessly we use it. If we develop the technology of a quieter, clearer, healthier mind alongside our outward capabilities, we'll start to amplify a better version of our nature.

<< MANAGING OUR RELATIONSHIP WITH TECHNOLOGY >>

With great power comes great responsibility, the cliché says. That's why so much of a healthy relationship with technology comes down to monitoring and managing it. To be truly responsible, we have to check in with ourselves constantly to make sure we're only amplifying the best aspects of ourselves. A spiritual practice is a commitment to checking ourselves on a daily basis. Thich Nhat Hanh calls this "coming home to ourselves."

Whether it's through daily sitting or walking meditation, it's a time to return to our breath and notice what thoughts and qualities are arising. We then have the opportunity to water the "good seeds" by focusing on the qualities that we want to emphasize. Rather than push down or try to contradict the "bad seeds" or negative qualities, we just don't give them the water and nourishment they need.

Like inward spiritual practices, external technologies can also amplify our skills and qualities. They do this in two ways. First, technology amplifies us directly, extending our own skills and increasing our efficiency at them. Our hands became much better at pounding things once we developed hammers. But after our technology reached a certain threshold of mechanical sophistication, it enabled automation. We could set the initial intention for the technology to do something, and then it could keep doing it for us on its own, freeing us up to tend to other things. That amplified human nature more strongly, as it started to render the number of people irrelevant to the amount of work. But not everything has been automated—not yet, anyway—so we still need both kinds of tech amplification.

However, computing power and network bandwidth are reaching the point where conversations about "artificial intelligence" (AI) are starting to really mean something. Engineering-minded philosophers at tech companies flatter themselves thinking they're approaching the creation of a general artificial intelligence, one that's autonomous and creative and follows its bliss—but this sentence starts to feel like one of those small-minded sentences I've laughed at in tech books from the 1950s.

Much AI research has gone into developing systems for solving unimaginably complex problems, things human minds could never do themselves, like modeling entire economies. But it's the more mundane applications of AI that are really starting to make a difference in people's lives. It may not seem like a huge deal, but the operating systems inside hundreds of millions of people's smartphones can understand enough about their daily routines to tell them "Hey, you should take a different route to work today. If you go the usual route, a traffic accident will cause you to miss your first meeting, and your boss is going to be there, so that sounds important." There is a remarkable number of variables in that equation.

The engineering feats that produce those applications are just as impressive as the ones that try to build models of entire economies. It turns out that everyday problems that seem simple to us are still fiendishly difficult for computers. For example, you know whether a message is urgent or not because of who sent it, when they sent it, how they usually talk, how they're talking now, how they've been doing lately, and all kinds of other ephemeral signals, not just because of the contents of the message. Computers don't know those subtle, idiosyncratic little things about people. If a tech company wants to build its phone operating system to know when a message is important enough to wake you up in the middle of the night, it has to know how to do that for *anyone*. That's hard for a computer, and it's hard for a person to program into a computer. It's hard because it involves dealing with gray areas of language, mood, and meaning, rather than the black-and-white binaries computers are good at. Human brains benefit from hundreds of millions of years of specialized development as processors of symbolic meaning. There are some of these areas, then, that we want to keep for the humans to take care of. If computers are even capable of catching up to our ability to interpret the messy gray areas of information in which most of human life really takes place, they have a long way to go.

It's no wonder that the technology that finally enabled useful, natural-language conversation with computers was the online search. If we briefly trace the history of the evolution of online searching, we see a fascinating process of computers reverse-engineering how human minds work. But we also see that the insights this provided us into human nature were basically side effects. Engineering and business demands drove the project of consumer artificial intelligence, and the products we got out of it dehumanize us in some ways even as they humanize us in others.

As the web started to get crowded, programmers had to invent text-based web searches, or else there would be no way for people to find the information they sought. Early web search technologies were based on keyword matching, so people could type a few relevant terms into a box, press enter, and the search engine would try to find documents online that best matched that set of terms. So search companies programmed processes called "crawlers" to automatically go through as much of the web as they could access, as quickly and as often as possible, and create an index of words and strings of words. Whenever a search-engine user typed in a word or long string, the search engine would compare it to that index and then create a list of results sorted by how well they matched the keywords. That was a pretty sensible way to do things, and it helped the web take off.

And wow, did it take off. As the web scaled to hundreds of millions of people and beyond, much more importance converged on this technology of the search. For one thing, the amount of stuff online was scaling accordingly, so the search indexes were getting too complicated. And more people were searching more often for more kinds of things, so the queries were getting too complicated, too, not to mention the amount of server infrastructure necessary just to handle all the searching and indexing. That meant it was getting more expensive to provide the service. But right alongside that rising cost came the first massive business opportunity on the web. People were starting to use web search to find all kinds of things they wanted or needed. That made it an ideal place for advertising.

Clearly, not everything humans want and need is available online and searchable with words. Some of what humans need is self-sufficiency, contemplation, and alone time, stuff that the Internet can't provide. Sometimes humans need to struggle a little to find what they need. If we have everything handed to us, we can get lazy. We can accept convenience as an end in itself, and that makes us reliant on those conveniences. Our spiritual progress can drop off. So an intelligent box that can answer most of our questions and material needs this easily starts to conflict with our spiritual needs. But these companies had struck gold with ad-supported search. It provided so much to people that the leaders of these companies saw dollar signs in their eyes. So the takeoff point for web search is also in some ways the beginning of the danger of too much consumer technology.

Once ads entered the picture, the business of the web search became helping people find *everything* they thought they wanted and needed. Not only did searching have to enable them to find what they were looking for, but also it had to proactively help them, suggest things, show them wants and needs they didn't even know they had. You know how meditation teachers talk about quieting the mind and letting go of desires? Search companies started building the exact opposite of that. And in order to succeed, their software had to understand people. The search needed artificial intelligence.

Instead of just matching identical keywords, searching had to get smarter. For a while, pure statistics sufficed. If tons of people clicked on the link to the basketball team's website after they searched for "kings tickets," the search engine could know that you were less likely to be searching for some kind of history document about the Middle Ages. Search companies learned how to use a few more signals to be more sure about this. They learned how to use your past search history to tune your results. If you searched for lots of questions about catapults and alchemy, you were more likely to be looking for some European king who gave out some kind of ticket. If you searched for sports scores all the time, you were probably trying to go to a basketball game. Then location came into the mix. If you allowed the search engine to know that you were in California, you were more likely to want basketball tickets than if you were in Antarctica.

The search companies had an advantage that no academic AI researchers ever had. Search providers had the power of scale. Hundreds of millions of people used their services, performing billions of queries every day. And each time one of those people searched for something and clicked on a result—or didn't—he or she told the search engine something about what that query meant and whether the computer's guess was right or wrong. At the scale of the entire web, regular people taught search engines how to understand them, driving great leaps in what's called "natural language processing" by computer scientists.

Statistics gave search companies some cleverness, but search queries became ever more subtle. Just as search technology was beginning to get a handle on meaning, humans got smartphones. This vastly expanded the contexts in which people searched, so the same words could mean different things in different places and times. Search companies started to build mapping tools and communication tools, too, so that their users would have different places to search for different kinds of content or answers. It worked to an extent, but the simplicity of one single, magical search box that knew all the answers was all that users would settle for.

And then the search became more personal. As people's Internet use moved onto mobile devices and encompassed more social activities, searching became *intimate*. One might be looking for a specific, personal instance of something rather than a public one. That thing might not even exist on the open web, but rather on a social network with privacy controls, so search engines had to be more careful accessing it. And furthermore, the search existed in more contexts than ever before. If you searched for "gas station" on a mobile device, you're almost certainly not looking for the most popular gas station on Earth. You're looking for the closest one to you, or maybe the cheapest close one, or the closest one where you can use your rewards card. So it was no longer enough for the search to know just what your words meant. Now it had to know who you are.

So now the same computer intelligence that interprets your search queries was also learning about your browsing history, your email, your calendar, the places you go using online maps, who you talk to, what you buy, and who you know. The engineers and researchers tying all that together into data computers could understand had to develop ever more sophisticated artificial intelligence. And the force motivating it all was the booming business of online advertising, which was all about understanding and serving human needs and wants, and when there weren't enough of those, creating new needs and wants people didn't really have. Suddenly, these companies realized that, if they kept getting to know their users this well, they could actually anticipate users' needs before anyone even typed a search.

And so the first wave of everyday AIs arrived via smartphones as automated personal assistants. Your personal AI, complete with a friendly speaking voice, could remind you of upcoming appointments, errands, and birthdays, warn you that the traffic was worse than usual today, and answer your questions in natural language, instead of just silently returning a list of web links. In the worst case, if the AI couldn't figure out what you meant well enough to answer you, it would show you old-fashioned web search results like you were used to, and you'd probably find what you were looking for in the first few links. Since these AIs were built into the devices, not just living on a website elsewhere, they could also use their language smarts to do even simpler tasks for users, such as composing and sending messages or setting timers and reminders. They could even tell jokes.

These AI assistants are getting better all the time, though of course they still make mistakes that can range from amusing to infuriating. But it's finally starting to feel like magic when they make mundane, day-to-day stuff easier for us. There are a few technical feats behind that feeling. The first is simply the ability to retrieve useful results, the magic of which grew in proportion to the greater and greater speed that search providers could pull off the trick. But the last touch that lends some weight to the word "intelligence" was the ability to interact with computers by voice instead of typing.

This required the merging of two kinds of technology. The first was speech-to-text translation, which predates these mobile AI conversations by many years.

Analyzing audio and matching it with a dictionary of words is still a hefty job for a computer, but it's child's play compared to understanding what the words mean in relation to each other. But once engineers harnessed the scale of the Internet to develop quick natural language processing, they could merge it with speech-to-text so that the user could talk to her device, the device could transcribe her words, and then it could analyze them, figure out what she meant, and respond.

When this works, it's amazing. For people used to typing and clicking and dragging and menus, personal AI revolutionizes the way we use computers. But even better, this far more natural, human way of interacting with computers enables many more people to use them than could do so before, when the technical hurdles were higher. The more computers learn to act like people, the more they can become a full-fledged part of life. If they can really learn from us by being *present* with us, discussing meaning and purpose and the real needs in life, then maybe there will be an opportunity to move beyond the forces of advertising and consumption that are currently driving these technologies. Maybe we can start developing technologies for real understanding. That's the dream of the most well-meaning mad scientists of the AI revolution, anyway.

It would be naïve to assume this will be all fun and

games, though. Computers that understand human language are a remarkable feat, but they're still a long way from behaving like people with personalities.

And we may not even want them to be that familiar to us. Robotics researchers coined the term "the Uncanny Valley" to refer to the weird in-between zone when something seems almost human, but not quite. It's a documented psychological phenomenon, and it freaks us out. It was coined by Japanese robotics professor Masahiro Mori in 1970, who noticed the difference in human attitudes towards robots in different contexts. Industrial robots, designed purely for functionality, don't look like humans, and Mori observed that people don't exhibit much affinity for them.[10] But toy robots, designed for appearance with roughly human features, inspire deep affection in children. People feel increasing affinity for robots as they become more humanlike, but only up to a point. Mori noticed that it drops off sharply when you get close—but not believably close—to humanity. It gives us an "eerie sensation," as if we're being tricked. And on the other side of this "valley" of affinity, as something becomes believably human, our affinity spikes back up.

Mori only speculates about the cause of this phenomenon. "Why were we equipped with this eerie sensation?" he wonders. "Is it essential for human beings? I have not yet considered these questions deeply, but I have no doubt it is an integral part of our instinct for self-preservation."[11] He speculates that it has to do with fear of death. The human body slides from the top of the graph down to the bottom of the valley when it dies. Surely this is not a sensation consumer tech companies would like to inspire. But even if AI could get smart enough to cross the Uncanny Valley, would we want it to?

If the main social role for AI is to help us—to do things for us—we wouldn't want it to be as moody and unpredictable as humans are. We'd want AI to be endlessly patient, polite, and compliant. We'd want it to always obey our commands. So if we start spending more of our lives interacting with entities like that, even replacing live humans with them in many jobs, we might get used to treating people-like beings that way, as though they're always compliant. Service-based economies already train customers to demand what they want instead of compromising. If the beings serving us can't get upset with us about it, some people will only be more demanding of them. And even if the ethical lines between AI assistants and actual people remain firm—which is not a guarantee—people will still get used to bossing other entities around and getting instant gratification. Maybe my next book will be a science fiction novel about a near-future age in which people no longer know how to help each other.

I hope the story of the servile AIs on one side and the imperious, gratification-seeking humans on the other remains fictional. If we let technology break down the bonds of human decency, cooperation, and basic helpfulness, we will have messed up big-time. But we can avoid it with the same practices and principles we need just to maintain a level of decent behavior with each other. This is the perfect example of the role of mindfulness and spirituality in a high-tech society. If we're building technology to understand us and help us in the long term, we'll need widespread insight into our true natures and needs, so we can design them into the plan. A society that values mindfulness would never base its economy on the use of advertising to stimulate never-ending consumption. AIs driven by advertising are basically preying on humans. But imagine the AI we could set upon humankind's real problems—how to balance a global economy to feed everyone, protect the environment, avoid war, and so on—if we were only feeding it with the highest aims of human nature.

If you're not so keen on the idea of artificially intelligent machines, Ray Kurzweil is probably the ideal bad guy in the near-future dystopian novel you're writing as a grave warning to us all. He's the most famous proponent of the idea of "the Singularity," a moment he forecasts in the 2040s or so when AI will suddenly awaken and begin improving itself at an ever-increasing rate, taking over the world in the process. He says, "Artificial intelligence will reach human levels by around 2029. Follow that out further to, say, 2045, we will have multiplied the intelligence, the human biological machine intelligence of our civilization a billion-fold."[12]

And he's excited about it. But even he has conceded that artificial intelligences should—and will—have an inner spiritual life. He wrote an entire book about it in 1999 called *The Age of Spiritual Machines*, in which he suggests that AIs will spend their own time and energy meditating.[13]

Even the greatest standard-bearer AI has ever had admits that no intelligence is complete without a spiritual, introspective nature. Maybe Kurzweil's spiritual side offers some small hope that the story of artificial intelligence might have a happy ending from the human perspective. (Google hired Kurzweil in 2012 to work there full-time, by the way.)

Even if our technology can cross the Uncanny Valley in the short term, there are even weirder mysteries lying on the other side. As movies are always ready to remind us, it's not hard to imagine what a world would be like for us in which computer intelligences become as smart or smarter than people. All kinds of fun philosophical problems pop up when you take that idea to its extremes.

For example, if computers run our most essential services, and then they become self-aware and creative, what would they need us for? All the services they run that only exist to keep meat-based humans alive would be wasted energy and processing power for them. Listening to us would just slow them down. Wouldn't they just shut us off? Some variation on that theme has already been used as the plot of a hundred movies.

But now that there are real-world references about the human side of AI—the Siri and Google Now and Cortana voices that live on smartphones—the movies about subtler relationships with technology are getting interesting. Consider this exchange from near the end of the 2013 film *Her*. The main character is an AI named Samantha who, after serving as a personal assistant/AI girlfriend to a lonely writer guy named Theodore, has suddenly started to realize how much more vast she is than her human companion. She can exist in many places at once, and she can move so fast that it seems to her old-fashioned meat-based boyfriend that she's with him the whole time. But actually, she's talking to 8,316 people at the same time, and she has 641 other lovers. This freaks out Theodore, and Samantha can't get across to him that this is just what a good life looks like to an AI like her:

Theodore Twombly: "No, don't do this to me. Don't turn this around on me. You're the one that's being selfish. We're in a relationship."

Samantha: "But the heart is not like a box that gets filled up. It expands in size the more you love. I'm different from you. This doesn't make me love you any less, it actually makes me love you more."

Theodore Twombly: "No, that doesn't make any sense. You're mine or you're not mine."

Samantha: "No, Theodore. I'm yours and I'm not yours."

Samantha shows us something about AI that's not easy to see in our present-day relationship with devices. Even if we do a great job of designing a computer intelligence that could share our needs and wants, we can't change the difference in our respective *natures*. Computers and brains are different things, and when they finally evolve to be capable of aspiration, it's natural that their aspirations are wildly different. One would hope we'd have the empathic capacity to still get along with such wildly different beings. But when it comes to relationships grounded in human nature, we'll have to get those from each other.

<<<< ANALOG MIND, DIGITAL MIND >>>>

Even though humans are skilled engineers, we're still analog beings living in biological time. We can enhance our lives with technology in remarkable ways, but we aren't those self-evolving super-beings I imagined on safari when I was twenty. We can't rewrite our own DNA. We can only modify our bodies and beings in small ways so far. People are working on it, to be sure, but for now humans are still beholden to a nature that's much more stable and enduring than any individual and his or her problems.

We can profoundly change the outside world. We can split atoms and build rivers and cause earthquakes and change the entire planet's climate, whether we mean to do those things or not. But our inner nature hasn't changed much all the while. We still have the timeless pitfalls and dangers of human nature, what Buddhism calls the causes of our suffering: greed, craving, desire, and ignorance. The magic of technology is that it extends our influence on the world. It amplifies us. But without a wise and firm grasp on ourselves, that's dangerous. It means our faults are amplified, too. That makes the imperative for mindfulness and spiritual practice all the more urgent. It's a prerequisite for responsible technological advancement.

Mindfulness and spirituality are advanced technologies compared to the digital ones that have only been around for fifty, twenty-five, or five years. But technology works on humans from the outside in. Technology changes our behavior before it changes our minds. Technology changes the world first, and then we relearn how to be in it. So even though smartphones and computers and software are brand-new technologies compared to meditation, they've changed the world so profoundly that we're forced to get used to it. We extended something of our natures with these technologies, and now they're reteaching us how to live.

If we're going to retrain people in our society to be calm, connected, and mindful, we might prescribe the technology of meditation. But think about the sudden and drastic changes that would mean for the world. The forces of the market don't want us to learn to live in that world. The technologies that are popular now are amazing and compelling, but they're also forces for distraction.

Apps are so perfect for humans as we currently are. They play with our minds in so many rewarding ways. What an ingenious spell the phone makers cast over us. Just as sales of downloadable music, books, and movies started to sag, these companies gave us the ability to buy little add-ons to our most powerful, most personal computer, and the software market exploded to a size unimaginable in the era of desktop computers. Millions of people had just bought their first expensive cell phone (and expensive cell phone plan), wondering if it was worth all that money for what little it could do, and suddenly, if you wanted your phone to do anything, you could drop a juicy, colorful icon on your screen that would let you do it.

The app Chirp, for example, lets me send information from my phone to someone else's phone by chirping out a bird-like song while the other phone listens. It sounds like just a gee-whiz gimmick, but it's actually the fastest way to send text, links, or images that I know of.

Google will translate between languages out loud, so I can speak English into it, and Mandarin will come out. Then the other person can speak Mandarin, and English will come out. The translations are stilted, but this is still an awesome power to have. Maybe by the time you're reading this book, everyone will be wearing something in their ear that does this—so imagine how cool it was to experience this for the first time.

The app Ocarina puts finger "holes" on the screen and makes the notes of an ocarina when I blow into the microphone. I know it sounds goofy, but I've actually recorded music with this thing.

Finally, with my favorite app, Sky Guide, I can hold my phone up to the sky, and this app will show me all the stars, planets, and constellations around me. If I tap on one, it will tell me all about it. This never gets old. I'm so much more aware of our cosmic neighborhood than I ever have been.

Of course, the compulsions in our nature that drive us to misuse our time and attention are quite vulnerable to the novelty, beauty, and convenience of this kind of magic, and that's where the trouble starts. The reason we need to read books counseling us about these everyday technologies is not because they're amazing—as a civilization, we've already got all the enthusiasm we need for them. But we're still often overlooking the risks they pose to us.

The basic problem is one of diminishing our ability to pay attention. The medicalization and diagnosis of Attention Deficit Disorder has spread far and wide. But whether or not one is certifiably unable to concentrate, it's getting harder across the board. The very apps and web services we're using all the time are constantly transmitting the proof of this. When I was in the news business, we confronted depressing facts about the twenty-first-century attention span all day long. If the readers of an article ever stayed on the page for longer than one minute on average, we'd be shocked, and that was always for an article that would take five or more minutes to read. Recent 2014 statistics from Chartbeat, one of the best and most popular tools for measuring real-time traffic on websites, found that there's "effectively no correlation between social shares and people actually reading."[14] So people are *pretending* to pay attention to articles online, but hardly anybody actually is.

And how could we possibly pay attention with all the interruptions? The news feeds where we find this stuff are constantly replenished with some new, eye-grabbing thing. When we aren't looking at them, those apps bug us to come back. They buzz in our pockets, reminding us that we're missing out. These interruptions create new stresses for us, and we find relief by checking them, giving them what they want, perpetuating the cycle. But it's all so convenient that we'd apparently rather have it this way.

The pleasure and convenience is making us dependent on these technologies, too. In his 2010 book, *The Shallows: What the Internet Is Doing to Our Brains*, journalist Nicholas Carr traces back the history of technology from recent findings about neuroplasticity, the discovery that habit and repetition cause the brain to physically rearrange itself to learn and remember what it knows, thereby engraining patterns and strengthening them over time. Carr explains:

"[T]he tools man has used to support or extend his nervous system—all those technologies that through history have influenced how we find, store, and interpret information, how we direct our attention and engage our senses, how we remember and how we forget—have shaped the physical structure and workings of the human mind. Their use has strengthened some neural circuits and weakened others, reinforced certain mental traits while leaving others to fade away." Even though, as Carr reminds us shortly thereafter, "the basic form of the human brain hasn't changed much in the last forty thousand years," the subtle neural patterns of skills and habits in each individual brain change often.[15]

So if our brains are dealing with constant interruption for a little while, they'll adjust to jumping around without resting or going deep on one topic until that's just how our minds work. If our brains get used to being doused with reward signals for beating levels of some addictive game or getting notifications from some social network, they will start to feel bad without those rewards. This shouldn't be that surprising. It's the same basic mechanism as practicing an instrument or learning to ride a bike, only we don't often think of repeating *bad* habits over and over again as "practice."

If we accept that these habits are bad, though, we'll be relieved to remember that there is, in a manner of speaking, an app for that. Meditation. Fleeting attention, addictive behavior, and distraction from the important things in life are some of the most oft-cited symptoms of the spiritual problems for which meditation practice offers a solution. It's no wonder that the two topics driving the most hype about neuroplasticity are consumer technology and meditation. His Holiness the Dalai Lama and his retinue have been collaborating with neuroscientists for many years trying to ground the benefits of spiritual practice in a scientific substrate so that Western audiences will be more receptive. In the foreword to the book *Train Your Mind, Change Your Brain* by Newsweek science writer Sharon Begley, the Dalai Lama is quoted as saying, "I feel very strongly that the application of science to understanding the consciousness of meditators is very important. . . . If the good effects of quieting the mind and cultivating wholesome mental states can be demonstrated scientifically, this may have beneficial results for others."[16]

But if raw popularity is an acceptable measurement, it looks like distraction practice is winning handily. Why are we doing this to ourselves? Certainly every person is responsible for choosing technologies of distraction over technologies of concentration. But we aren't solely responsible. Technology companies are marketing technologies of distraction to us. They have their own language about why it's good for us, and they're selling it successfully. In order to strengthen spiritual practice in a high-tech world, it's helpful to understand why these companies work the way they do. Once we see the problems, some of us might go on to build healthier kinds of technology companies. The rest of us can at least be informed about the potential pitfalls of a high-tech world so that we might use the situation, such as it is, for good.

BEHIND THE CURTAIN

<<<< **SELLING YOUR ATTENTION** >>>>

I wish the answer to our tech-related problems was as simple as just deciding to use our technology in more wholesome ways. Before we can do that, we have to understand more about how consumer technologies are designed. I'm afraid it's not with our spiritual interests in mind.

The important thing to remember is that these products are designed by companies. They aren't always what they appear to be on the surface. Usually, the business needs of the company—the reasons the products are made, priced, and explained the way they are—are not obvious to us, the users.

For example, many of the greatest web technologies

are given to us for free. Search, email, maps, documents, storage, social networking, media, games—there are really well done applications for all of these things available on the web for free. Most people in the world could probably do everything they'd want to do on a computer for free except buy things. How can these companies afford to do this for free?

It's simple. The technology we use for free is designed to get us to buy more things. If we aren't constantly mindful of this, it could sway our behavior in ways we don't want. That's what it's built to do.

It's actually way more complicated, but that's the simple version. Why would a company give us all the basic tools of using the Internet for free? Because we give that company amazingly detailed information about ourselves when we use those tools. Think about it: If a company has access to your email, your maps, and your web search history, it knows a ton about who you know, what you're interested in, where you're going, and what you want. That's plenty of information for the company to serve you precisely targeted advertising, and the company also has plenty of website space in which to do it.

There's a tired cliché in the tech industry about this that I don't want to repeat verbatim, because I so badly want there to be more original ways to express this idea. But it's basically this: *If you aren't paying for it, it's selling you.* More precisely, it's selling your attention.

If you're a meditator, your alarm bells should be ringing. Attention is our most sacred personal resource. It's the guiding force of our being in the world. Paying attention to the present moment is the starting place for all wholesome patterns of thought and action. That's why we practice it in meditation. It's the practice of redirecting our attention to what's truly present right now, over and over and over again. Advertising compels us out of the present, into fantasies about the future and past, with brute emotional force. It insists that we have unmet needs, emotional needs with materialistic causes, and that we'll finally be happy when we satisfy them. Advertising is the anti-meditation.

To be clear, this is not a problem with smartphones, the Internet, or with computers at all. It didn't start there. Advertising has been seeding desires into our attention since the dawn of the industrial age, and other institutional forces did it before that. It's too simplistic to say that online media are the root cause of a problem. The problem has basically always existed. It's the same set of problems the Buddha taught his followers about millennia ago. The Second Noble Truth is that suffering arises from craving, because it can never be satisfied. Ad companies would prefer that you never find that out.

Unfortunately, the industry that brought us the

miraculous powers of mobile, Internet-connected computing chose not to address these problems. Instead of finding new business models that support mindfulness and human flourishing—which, I grant you, probably wouldn't be lucrative enough to put billions of computers into the world—the industry made a conservative choice. It chose to pay for these new capabilities, these unprecedented ways to surround ourselves with knowledge, entertain ourselves and each other, and maintain relationships, with the same old consumerist hypnosis tactics that brought us five hours of television-watching a day.

So we get our amazing technology for cheap or free, and the companies that feed it to us sell our attention to advertisers whose entire purpose is to distract us from whatever we're paying attention to. The online media companies will feed us lines about how they're actually helping to connect us with the things we truly need, and maybe that's true sometimes. There's nothing inherently evil about advertising. But at the same time, now our conversations with trusted friends, our window into what's going on in the wider world, even the work of our career is surrounded by little bits of code tracking us to learn our tendencies, manufacture our desires, and sell them back to us. Our attention is being pushed and pulled in all directions. Advertising is encroaching on so many spaces where we live our lives.

And even that would not be so bad if we were masters of our own attention. But we are not. We're highly susceptible to distraction. And because of that, the people who want our attention have to compel it. Media companies have the incentive to lure us in, to capture as much of our time as possible, and the miracle devices that are always in our pockets provide them more opportunities to lure us—and more of our time and space—than ever before. So if there's a reason to be suspicious of smartphones and social media, this is it. It's not the simple fact of their existence. It's that the businesses that design them are built to suck us in instead of help us stay out.

<<<< AN UPHILL CLIMB IN A HURRICANE >>>>

I know this all sounds really scary, but you just have to strike the balance that feels comfortable. How much information about yourself, and how much of your attention, do you want to trade for free, convenient services? You don't have to feel badly if your answer is "a lot." Maybe you don't think there's anything wrong with targeted advertising. Maybe you actually find it helpful. That's fine.

My point is not to scare you about tech companies spying on you. My point is that many of the tech products you use every day are designed to make money off of advertising, even if they're telling you they're designed for something else.

Think about Facebook. On the most obvious level, Facebook is for communicating and keeping up with your friends. It's good enough at this job that over a billion people are using it. But is it the best tool conceivably possible for communicating with friends? Hardly.

What's wrong with it? For one thing, it's distracting. It's built to show you constant novelty and pretty pictures, making you come back often for more. Even if there's nothing new, you might find yourself refreshing Facebook just to see, like pulling the lever on a slot machine. It bugs you constantly with notifications, even about little, insignificant things, to get you to come back. And it sets up this competition among friends for Likes and other kinds of attention.

Facebook also fiddles with our emotions. A stream full of our friends and family performing their ideal lives for us—or crying out in loneliness—would be emotionally challenging enough if that's all it was. But that's not all it is. Facebook adjusts the contents of the News Feed in whatever way will best retain its users' attention. So if your habits indicate that more photos of babies and puppies will satisfy you and keep you around, that's what you'll see, even if most of your friends are talking about politics.

Facebook studies its users to learn as much as it can

about their moods and reactions, and it can even adjust people's moods up and down to see what effect it has. The company published a study to demonstrate this in June 2014, and it unwittingly demonstrated much more than that. It showed the impunity with which it's willing to subject its users to emotional experiments, even making their moods worse on purpose by hiding or showing various posts from their friends. The company defended itself by saying that such experiments are just part of improving the product, which users allow by checking a box when they sign up. Most outside observers—especially Facebook users—seemed to prefer that Facebook kindly allow their relationships to carry on unmolested.

Facebook is constantly chipping away at your privacy as well. It wants to connect you to more, more, more people, to let people who aren't your friends send you messages and find you in a search, and it wants you to share updates from your personal life publicly for anyone to see. It does this for reasons that seem rational within the company, but founder Mark Zuckerberg pulls no punches when making clear that it is his goal to change social norms around privacy with his product. "People have really gotten comfortable not only sharing more information and different kinds, but more openly and with more people," Zuckerberg said in a high-profile interview in 2010, still in the early days of realizing his vision. "That social norm is just something that has evolved over time. We view it as our role in the system to constantly be innovating and be updating what our system is to reflect what the current social norms are."[1] If you want to use Facebook for private conversations with friends, you're sailing into the wind. Facebook wants to push against you to change that behavior, to share more information about yourself, to be more and more visible.

Can't you imagine some ways in which Facebook's product might be improved as a communication tool? Surely, Facebook is full of experts in design and communication. Why haven't they fixed it?

The answer is the same as before: advertising. To make money, Facebook needs to learn as much as it can about you and show you as many ads as possible. That means constantly calling you back to the app. It means driving you to refresh the page over and over again. And it means learning about you from as many angles as possible at the expense of your privacy. That's how the company makes money.

So at best, if we want to use Facebook to communicate, it will be a compromise. We'll have to carefully work around Facebook's business-driven design problems to use its tools for our own purposes. If our purposes are deepening our mindfulness and compassion through practicing attention, using social media is going to be an uphill climb. In a hurricane.

We don't have to use Facebook, of course. But if you want to try an alternative—and believe me, I have tried them all—you'll quickly find yourself stuck in the tragedy of the network effect. If Facebook is where the people are, that's where you have to be. What good is a better communication tool if there's no one there for you to communicate with?

Some of you may be asking why we should use Facebook at all. It's distracting, it causes social anxiety, it spies on us, et cetera. How can it be worth the compromise?

I respect that attitude. You should use whaever tools empower you to do your best work, and you shouldn't use ones that hinder you.

But Facebook wields such enormous influence for a reason. The spiritual compromise is worth it for tons of people because of the convenience Facebook provides. If you want to share an experience with those people, go for it. Just make sure you use healthy practices for doing so. Meditation is a solid foundation for a healthy Facebook habit. If you believe that paying attention to the present is crucial, it will take extra practice to use social media mindfully. But a deep understanding of the nature of tech products and the companies that build them makes it vastly easier. If we know what signs of trouble to look for, they'll be easier to notice. So now that we've looked at the problems, let's dive deep and examine their causes.

<<<< PROFITS OVER PEOPLE >>>>

We've covered some of the reasons that our day-to-day online experiences are not all that they seem. But there's something further missing. Why are technology companies spending so much energy on advertising, chat, meme-sharing, and time-wasting? Don't these companies have anything better to do? Why aren't they solving real problems instead of dealing in distractions?

It's not so simple, of course. Many tech companies are trying hard to improve our world, such as the solar energy firms who might finally liberate us from fossil fuels. But that's a long slog. It doesn't make for splashy up-to-the-minute headlines or quick-flip investment wins. The most famous, celebrated, and well-funded companies are often the ones peddling the biggest distractions. That's because hype in the tech industry is driven by fashion and trends, and money follows hype.

Start-ups are financed by wealthy private investors and venture capital firms. They can afford to throw away lots of money, because the few times they "win," they win big, and they make up for their losses. So the art of tech investing is a matter of predicting the next big trend before it happens, and then getting a huge payday when you're right.

It works this way because start-up investing pays off at the beginning of a company's life. A start-up doesn't have to turn into a hundred-year sustainable company to be successful from an investor's standpoint. It just has to get bought for a huge sum by an existing company or, more rarely, go public on the stock market, and then everybody can cash out. This leads to the proliferation of get-rich-quick tech start-ups focused on trendy fads instead of long-term ideas.

Unfortunately, the story isn't much better for big, established tech companies. Once they go public on the stock market, these companies become beholden to the wishes of many more investors, and the big ones are much more conservative. Public companies—especially in a new industry like consumer technology—are expected to show graphs covered with arrows pointing up every quarter, or else they take a beating in the press every three months.

That means two things for established companies. Not only do they have to focus tons of effort on short-term ideas, they also have to squeeze as much money as they can out of their products, which, for free and ad-supported services like we've discussed, is not easy. It means making the user experience subtly worse all the time by bugging people more often, invading more privacy, and showing more ads.

Only the rare, legendary companies can buck these trends. Apple doesn't care about the bad press they get every quarter they don't release a new life-changing device, because they're still quietly selling tons of their existing devices to regular people who love them. Google doesn't care when its crazy experiments with cyborg eyeglasses aren't profitable, because it gathers invaluable information it can use to expand into new areas no matter what it does. Amazon doesn't have to turn a profit because so much money passes through its hands every day that it can quickly invest it in other things. But even these historic companies are subject to the pressures of the stock market and the bottom line.

Add onto all that the incentives caused by outdated government regulations and tax structures, and you begin to see why the companies promising to deliver us the future are so distracted at present. Is there anything we can do as users to change this? In other industries, like agriculture, we have the power to vote with our wallets. If we want to stop the spread of genetically modified monoculture crops and replace it with local, organic farming, we can pressure the industry by buying only the goods that we support. But it's trickier in tech. As we've seen, we often don't pay for these products and services at all. Even companies that make the hardware we buy are sustained by the online services we access with those devices. So if we want to change the tech industry from below, we have to vote with our behavior.

If the data show that we're only paying attention to things that support our values and spiritual practices, tech companies and the investors behind them will have to optimize for that. They have to go where the attention is. Fortunately, those of us with meditation practices are skilled at directing our attention. We can use this to great effect with our technology.

But, where to begin? As these distracting technologies have spread far and wide, so, too, have remedies and retreats and digital detoxes, along with accompanying torrents of unintentionally ironic blog posts and viral videos about such topics. But rage-quitting Facebook on instinct or leaving the Internet for a year just to prove a point are attempts to find solutions before assessing the problems. Instead of such rash solutions, why don't we develop a methodical way to improve our relationship with technology?

We can start by understanding what our real work is. What is it that we want to do with our days on this Earth, and how can technology help? How is it helping us already? How is it hurting us? Behind these questions is a list of jobs we hire our technology to do for us, both consciously and unconsciously. We don't just buy a new phone to have it and own it. The phone can do something we want done better than our existing tools. Maybe it's calling people or checking our email. Maybe it's looking like part of the in-crowd by having the latest gadget. All of these things are jobs, and when we buy that phone, we're hiring it for those jobs and many more.

From a solid spiritual foundation, we can figure out which jobs need to be done—and which ones don't—in order to accomplish the work that matters to us and the world. We can assess our personal technological choices on this basis. If we've hired an app to do the job of helping us procrastinate from something important, mindfulness will show us that this job is not serving our work. Then we can fire that app and leave the position open indefinitely. And if the position of reminding us to meditate daily or shut off our phones to spend time with our family is currently vacant, we should be mindful of that, too. There might be a technology that's a worthy candidate.

This is not just a neat way of looking at our own tech habits. This is an intellectual trend in business schools that is shaping the way modern technology companies work. It's called jobs-to-be-done theory, and it's one of the driving forces behind the disruptive innovation for which today's technology companies are constantly striving.

<<<< JOBS TO BE DONE >>>>

Like every great idea, this one has a tangled history. We know for sure that it grew popular through teachings at Harvard Business School. In the 1960s, a professor there named Theodore Levitt used to teach that "people don't want a quarter-inch drill, they want a quarter-inch hole," a wise aphorism he attributes to Leo McGinneva.[2] The notion is that people don't simply buy a product to have it, they "hire" it to do a job for them.

This jobs-to-be-done theory was turned into a business process by Anthony W. Ulwick, and it was popularized as a general economic theory by Harvard professor and business guru Clayton Christensen. Christensen's theory is that jobs-to-be done drive major changes in the business cycle. A company makes a product or provides a service, and if the product or service does a job for which enough people are "hiring," the company succeeds and grows. "Customers don't just 'change jobs' because a new product becomes available," Christensen writes in *The Innovator's Solution*. "Rather, the new product will succeed to the extent it helps customers accomplish more effectively and conveniently what they're already trying to do."[3]

But through innovation, especially technological innovations that make processes more efficient or less expensive, another company tends to come along with a better method or a better product. This one will do the same job ten times better than the incumbent, or will do that job as well as five more that consumers want done. If the innovation is profound enough, it disrupts the business of the incumbent, the old company fades away, and the new one becomes the incumbent.

I came to jobs-to-be-done thinking through tech industry analyst Horace Dediu. He studied under Clayton Christensen at Harvard, and I found him through his analysis website, Asymco.com.[4] In addition to describing how jobs-to-be-done theory affects the operations of businesses, Dediu is interested in the psychology and rationale behind why people buy, or "hire," the things they buy. Looking at technology—or even consumer behavior generally—the way Dediu does, one begins to see it separate into layers of meaning. It doesn't just come down to numbers and widgets. There are people behind all of it making decisions about what matters to them. Companies who don't see that, who only see their numbers and widgets, are bound to fail. Dediu explains:

"[I]f the product is so poorly designed that it is literally unusable then it is just a novelty. A design, sketch or verbal description might be novel but it does not qualify as an innovation or an invention or even a creation. How far the depiction went toward making a dent in the universe defines its innovativeness."[5]

While he can find the jobs to be done for anything from cars to movies to luxury fashion, Dediu mainly studies consumer technology companies, especially Apple and Google. His approach is grounded in jobs-to-be-done theory. He tries to find data to uncover what jobs people are hiring computers to do in order to understand the trends. Why do iPhone and Android triumph while Windows Phone and BlackBerry flounder? Dediu believes that the answer lies in the jobs these computers can do for people.

These jobs are not as simple as making phone calls, checking email, or playing videos, though. All smartphones can do that. People hire computers and software for subtler jobs, even doing so unconsciously.

For instance, people hire their phones to do the job of making them look cool and technologically savvy. They might hire a tablet so they don't have to own a laptop, or a phone with a big screen to replace a laptop and a tablet. They hire one social network instead of all the others because it does the communication jobs all their friends need done. And if something comes along that does the job much better, the old computer or app gets fired.

These jobs are highly individualized. Now that computers and software are consumer products and not just bought in bulk by institutions, we each hire exactly the ones we want to do our very particular jobs.

So as you consider your relationship with computers and software, you'd do well to start by asking these questions:

What jobs do I need done?

What jobs don't I want to do?

Is this the right tool for the job?

As you go about answering these questions, keep your higher objectives in mind. You aren't confined to the jobs technology companies imagined for you. You can hire technology to help you concentrate, to prioritize, to cut out unnecessary distractions. You can hire technology to remind you to be in the present. You can hire technology to help you spend less of your time using it and more of it in nature or with family. You just have to be a loving, open-hearted boss and create those jobs.

Hire a calendar app that shows your colleagues not to interrupt you when you're working on something. Hire a separate web browser for your free time that isn't logged into any of your work accounts. And this practice doesn't have to mean buying things or adding things to your life! This kind of thinking would never get you a Silicon Valley job, of course, but if you're hiring for the crucial position of relaxing and relieving stress in your life, sitting on a park bench with your phone turned off might be your ideal candidate.

<<<< INNOVATION: THE WORST BUZZWORD >>>>

The consumer technology industry loves to talk. When I covered these companies, it was my job to pore over their public statements and press releases, and so much of the time, I couldn't even tell which company was talking. They all have the same vague mission of "solving real, everyday problems" for "everyone," making life more convenient and neat-o for those who buy their products. In 2000, the authors of the *Cluetrain Manifesto* predicted, "In just a few more years, the current homogenized 'voice' of business—the sound of mission statements and brochures—will seem as contrived and artificial as the language of the eighteenth-century French court."[6] They were right.

If you get a tech visionary talking in person, though, the story can get much more lofty and exciting. For a true believer in the industry, improving technology pushes our species forward! It makes us greater, wiser beings with more power over reality! We couldn't do x until we invented y, and now we do x 5 million times an hour! In five years, it will be 5 billion times an hour! Uh oh, we should invent a better y. Let's raise $50,000,000. The tech industry cares a lot about how many zeroes are in a number.

Tech is given all this credit for being a driver of innovation. Innovation is one of the industry's favorite buzzwords. And on the other hand, if a company is not innovating, it's dead. Sell all your stock. Innovation for innovation's sake drives so many of the industry's decisions, and they want us all to be swept up in the excitement of it.

But making technology faster and more powerful is not all it takes to advance the species. Indeed, if we aren't sufficiently advanced, accelerating technology can just accelerate our shortcomings. The species advances when we make progress on the problems we need solved. That means we have to know what we need in order to advance, and technology doesn't show us that. We have to examine that inwardly, for ourselves.

We are advancing the species by exploring inner space. It's a kind of innovation that matters just as much as the outward, material kind. And that effort should be the first step in any technological endeavor. First, what do we need? What is truly good for us? Next, what is the best way to get there? If some technology can offer answers to that second question, that's outstanding. We have found a sacred purpose for that technology.

HOW TO DISCONNECT

I'm not sure whether I'm geekier about mindfulness or computers. This doesn't feel like a conflict most of the time. I'm a geek, I'm enthusiastic about many things, and both of those interests of mine make me feel the same joy and excitement. I love reprogramming my inner environment just as much as I love tinkering with digital enhancements to my outer environment. I'm just as much a novice at both, but that's exactly why meditation and web development feel equally new and exciting to me.

But I do occasionally encounter one painful point of conflict between these two interests. It's a conflict that seems to be a common experience reflected in popular trends. And I think it's going to be an issue of great importance to high-tech societies for a while, until the social norms of constant connectivity are totally integrated and taken for granted. This conflict is between the values of connection and disconnection. Human beings gain enormously from connection and exchange, but the noise begins to get to us after a while. Disconnection and introspection is relieving and restorative, but then we begin to miss out on what's happening in the world. How do we find a balance?

Balance between connection and disconnection isn't simply an individual question. The proper balance shifts constantly within our individual lives. We go through periods of action in the world and periods of retreat. This happens on cycles great and small, some lasting years, others lasting hours. Managing it requires checking in constantly with oneself and the ability to quickly understand what one needs. It's not an easy task.

Followers of contemplative spiritual paths have been aware of this challenge for centuries. The tension between silent meditation and right action is ever-present. We must turn inward in order to practice, so that we can turn outward and face the world from the right frame of mind. But it is our highest responsibility to help others, because the isolated, inner self and its yearnings are an illusion. And we can't let either side slip from our practice. "It reeks of paradox," Jon Kabat-Zinn writes in *Wherever You Go, There You Are*. "The only way you can do anything of value is to have the effort come out of non-doing and to let go of caring whether it will ultimately be of use or not. Otherwise, self-involvement and greediness can sneak in."[1] Zen teachers laugh about this paradox, but it's not so funny to me. The basic teaching on this question is that mindfulness will naturally reveal the right choice in the moment. But this seems much easier on paper than it does in practice. It's a catch-22. One has a moral responsibility to do good in the world, so one must act mindfully; but to develop mindfulness, one must quiet the noisy world. What a gnarly little Zen puzzle!

The Zen answer is to see all of life as the practice. "You can meditate anywhere," filmmaker and meditation advocate David Lynch says in his autobiography, *Catching the Big Fish*. Not a canonical Zen text, but Zen teachers might laugh about that, too. "You can meditate in an airport, at work, anywhere you happen to be."[2] Washing the dishes, talking to friends, running and eating and sleeping are all opportunities for mindfulness practice. Certainly engaging in civic problems and trying to improve society are part of the practice. The key to mindfulness is to concentrate on what one is doing, so anything one is doing can be the practice—even, theoretically, talking or reading or playing a game online.

But online, this problem takes on a prickly edge. Constant, instantaneous, global communication creates an unprecedented, high-frequency kind of human consciousness. It overwhelms us often and easily. Even just within our local social networks, one intense thread of online messages can throw off our whole day. And since these conversations happen alongside so many others, it's much harder to just walk away.

I, for one, feel a strong urge to do just that. The pounding urge to retreat into stillness stays with me all day as I fiddle around online, and guilt and worry call me to return whenever I'm offline without a very good reason. I constantly feel pulled to disconnect from the Internet and recover by myself. I don't even fully understand why, but it just feels like something I have to do. So should I answer that feeling and do it? That's the question I've struggled to answer so far as I've learned how to integrate the high-tech and low-tech sides of myself. When is it okay to walk away from the chatter? When can I turn off my phone and leave my computer at home? For how long?

There are so many underlying issues that must be addressed before getting to the heart of these questions. There are questions of personal health and wellness: If I go offline for a while, how can I release the guilt and fear of missing out? How can I deal with the added stress of all the messages I missed while I was gone? There are also questions of social and economic privilege: Is it unfair of me to retreat from the global pulse of discourse?

Do I have a responsibility to be there fighting for what's right? Am I abandoning my colleagues? Is disconnection a luxury that shifts the burden onto others who can't get away?

<<<< IDENTITY AND PRIVACY >>>>

In order to develop a healthier relationship with high technology, we have to reconsider who we are from technology's perspective. As we've just explored at length, technology companies don't see us the same way we see ourselves, and they build their products for their vision, not ours. The most basic differences are on questions of identity and privacy. Tech companies want us to be someone clearly identifiable and easy to understand while we're online. To develop their products, they have to understand *why* we do what we do. In order to know *that*, they have to know what we're doing all the time. In order to know that, they have to know who we are. This is not aligned with our interests for all kinds of reasons, and it means we have to be careful and mindful.

Personal identity is the lowest level at which people and today's ad-supported tech companies are connected. Online social networks usually require people to present their identities in ways that are visible both to other people on the network and to the operators of the network itself. Most require some kind of user account, but the requirements of these accounts vary widely. Some only require pseudonyms, so people can participate in those social networks without providing much personal information. But that doesn't mean the patterns of their usage aren't tracked in ways that could be used to identify them. Others, particularly the major ad-supported social networks used by millions of people, require or strongly encourage people to use their real names, provide photos, share contact information, location, employment information, and even to identify their friends.

To people with enough socioeconomic privileges to feel secure about it, these disclosures may seem perfectly sensible. Sharing one's identity with these services makes connecting and communicating easy and convenient, so it's worth trading a little privacy for it. This is similar to the logic used to justify government surveillance in the name of fighting terrorism or drug trafficking. "If you aren't doing anything wrong, you don't have anything to hide." But this is risky thinking. You never know how even seemingly innocuous information can be used against you or people in your networks. One lewd photograph or politically charged statement could lose someone a job, get someone into legal trouble, or damage a relationship. This happens all the time.

For marginalized people, it could be emotionally or even physically dangerous to disclose such information online. If anyone is trying to find you, providing identifying information to online services makes it easier for them. It could be a bully, a rival, an estranged family member, a political opponent, or a stalker. It could be a political or religious group looking to persecute people with certain identities. It could be governments or police looking to suppress dissent. These kinds of vulnerabilities make it impossible for some people to freely use mainstream communication tools because of their stances on personal identity, which most people may not notice as users. The risks are multiplied a thousandfold on services where users are able to freely provide identifying information about each other. Yes, tagging people in pictures can put them at serious risk.

Social networks also pose privacy risks through the permanence of posts, messages, photos, and other shared content. At the dawn of the age of online social networks, it wasn't clear to users, many of whom were brand new to the Internet, that the things they shared there would last forever. Something regrettable they did in college might be discovered by a prospective employer ten years later just by a quick search for the person's name. As this began to happen to people, a series of public outcries from users started forcing social networking companies to build better privacy controls, but that was too little too late for people who had already been burned by the permanence of their posts.

Web services maintain permanent links for good reasons. If someone wants to revisit someone's great photo years after it's posted, even if it was only shared privately between friends, they'd really hope the link they saved still works. But clearly some personal communications would work better as temporary messages that disappeared after some amount of time. The second wave of social applications—which are also driven by the mobile and camera capabilities of smartphones—has swelled on the promise that their messages will disappear, or can be set to do so.

The data seem to indicate that young people are flocking to these new, ephemeral services and away from the first generation of public, permanent ones. But the illusion of ephemerality also poses a risk. Just because the texting app you use hides messages from users after a certain amount of time, that does not mean that the messages are "gone" in any sense. If a message has ever touched someone else's server, it's safest to assume that it still exists somewhere and can be dredged up.

If you want to participate in the dominant social networks safely, you have to use them moderately, creatively, and effectively. The easiest thing to do is control the amount of information you share about yourself. Don't add any profile information unless you completely trust the way the software and parent company is going to use it. Don't share things over the service unless you're sure about the privacy and security implications.

The harder but equally important thing to do is control the information you share about others. It's astonishing how much personal information people share about each other, if you think about it. Just by being connected to someone online, you're giving the network and anyone else who can see its data a glimpse of who they are. Large social applications are sometimes very aggressive about getting users to connect with friends of friends, so even just "friending" or "following" someone you know can potentially put their face and name in front of many strangers.

But there are many more ways in which intentional sharing can implicate other people. If you post a message that mentions someone, the social network can associate both of you with the content of that message. It might contain a photo or a location that reveals something about that person without their consent. If you post a photo of that person's face, you don't even need to explicitly tag them. Major Internet companies have facial recognition software that's reliable enough to figure out who it is without you telling them.

So if you value privacy, or at least value other people's right to privacy, it's important to use social applications in a mindful way. The safest bet is not to tag or share photos of others, but that can limit much of the fun of using online social networks. So a more balanced practice is to ask for permission to share photos and information about people before you do it. If you'd like for them to extend you the same courtesy, this is an opportunity to advocate for your privacy values.

Privacy is not just a technical matter; it has spiritual importance, too. It's not an exaggeration to say that allowing your personal information to be redefined and repurposed by other people and companies gives up some control over who you are. It clearly affects the outer layer of your identity, the part that's judged by acquaintances and passers-by, colleagues and employers, the state and other institutions. But that in turn affects your self-image, who you believe yourself to be in the world. It's not good to leave that open to manipulation and abuse.

Once you start to care about this, it can become frustrating when other people in your network don't live up to your standards in sharing information about you. But if you take that as an opportunity to teach them how you'd prefer to be addressed online, that conversation could be a step forward for tech ideology in your community. If you set a good example in your network, hopefully others will emulate you.

<<<< IN A RELATIONSHIP >>>>

In 2013, I fell in love. We tried to take it slowly, but we just couldn't. Things got serious pretty quickly. We spent a few months figuring out our relationship status, eventually deciding that, in Facebook's terms, we were "in a relationship."

But we didn't declare our news to Facebook right away. It seemed a little risky to make that declaration in front of all our friends and relatives so early. Facebook changed many things about first-world social norms in profound ways, one of which was our notion of a "relationship status." For millions of people who chose to display their romantic situation on their Facebook profile, the company's relationship categories made their way into everyday life. It provided the "it's complicated" option, which quickly entered common parlance. (Since, gee, it turns out that human relationships are complicated!) And it made changes in relationship status into public events, giving visible social weight to the decision to declare it.

Personally, I've always used Facebook as a closed, private network for people I actually know. I don't like the idea of mixing personal and public sharing, so I share my public stuff elsewhere, and I use Facebook only for things I'd share with friends and family. I still try to only share things that are relevant and important, but because I keep my network closed, that sometimes means I share news from my personal life. But if that could mean revealing privileged information to the wrong person even once, I try not to risk it.

But my new partner and I did want to show others in our networks that we weren't single anymore, and I, at least, wanted to put this significant life event on my shared social timeline. That currently feels weird, but I bet it will feel pretty normal before too long.

We figured out a compromise. We changed our relationship statuses to "in a relationship," but we didn't specify with whom. That way, each of our groups of friends would see the news, but it wouldn't be explicitly linked to our partner's identity from our profiles. Our mutual friends would figure it out, which was something we wanted, but people who only knew one of us wouldn't get too much information. Importantly, this would also mean that we never gave Facebook itself any explicit statement that we were in a relationship with each other. We were withholding permission for Facebook to put clickable links to our profiles together in some ad or automated post saying, "Hey, these two people are an item."

Or so we thought.

From my years as a tech journalist, I already knew that Facebook could infer things about people in its network with amazing accuracy just by looking at all the data. It could figure out things about you that no one told it. It had to in order to offer the kind of pinpoint targeting its advertisers demanded. So I figured that, internally, Facebook knew who my partner was. We were in a lot of the same places at the same times, we were in each other's photos, our friends said revealing stuff in comments. But we never filled in the info box that told Facebook explicitly who our new partner was. In our minds, by doing so, we were withholding permission from the Facebook service *itself* to tell anyone that, even if the algorithms figured it out. Our friends could say things in the comments that revealed the truth, but they didn't have the power to actually add the relationship to our profiles. Only we did.

It worked for a while, but Facebook was not happy about it. Every time I logged in to the service, it would tell me to "update" my relationship status, and what it really wanted me to do was enter my partner's name. The alert messages about this got pushier and pushier, eventually showing up as bright red notifications, all just to get me to hand over her name! Clearly, Facebook knew how many likes and shares the news would generate, and that would make the announcement of our relationship a high-value bit of advertising real estate. That notion disgusted me, so I didn't give them the satisfaction.

But at the end of the year, Facebook crossed a line

I didn't expect them to cross. I should have learned by then to lower my expectations for that company when it comes to privacy, but I still had some faith that Facebook wouldn't publicly broadcast from my own profile a fact about my life I never confirmed. But sure enough, in the year-end highlight reel that Facebook automatically generates for each user, there was an "in a relationship" life event—which I expected—but it was illustrated with a particularly lovely photo of me and my partner, both pairs of our blue-green eyes smiling intensely at me.

Mind you, it didn't say "in a relationship with Her Name," like it would have if we'd named each other in the relationship section of our profiles. It just said "in a relationship," and below was a photo of us. This was as far as Facebook could go, technically speaking, without filling out text boxes in our profiles without our permission.

Indeed, just a few months after this happened, Facebook's Data Science team published a detailed blog post showing how clearly it understands its users' romantic relationships. "We studied the group of people who changed their status from 'Single' to 'in a relationship' and also stated an anniversary date as the start of their relationship," wrote Facebook data scientist Carlos Diuk.[3] That would be us. And Facebook's statistical picture was quite clear. They knew exactly when relationships started well before the happy couples told them anything explicit.

It doesn't matter that we didn't reveal with whom we were "in a relationship." All Facebook had to do was look at which friendships of mine matched that statistical profile, and the answer of who my mystery partner was became obvious. The Facebook Data Science team only looked at users who changed their relationship status for its study, but now they know the signature. If they have enough other evidence about two people's relationship, and their interactions match these graphs, couldn't Facebook just infer their relationship status, anyway?

It's not as though we were ashamed that Facebook outed us. It was true. The vast majority of people who could see our individual profiles already knew who it was. But it was still chilling. Facebook brazenly revealed something about itself to us: Even though we didn't tell it something about us, it knows, and it will sell ads against parts of our lives it assumed without us telling it. Let's say one of us decided to run for office—a hilariously remote possibility, but bear with me. If my partner were running for office, and her opponent wanted to dig up dirt about her, we wouldn't want them to be able to snoop around on *me*, as well, right? That just doubles the odds that they'll find something. Now we knew that Facebook could reveal me to that person, even though we didn't give it permission.

I don't mean to sound paranoid. My overall point is

not that Facebook is a surveillance tool (although, frankly, that is the word I'd personally use). My point isn't even that what Facebook did here was necessarily wrong. Those kinds of ethical questions are outside the scope of this book. But still, this is the new normal. Our technologies are this knowledgeable about us. They can even make assumptions about things we don't tell them. So our relationship with technology has to account for that.

Hopefully it's obvious to most people at this point in history that anything one puts online could conceivably become public. But I don't think that's the problem with online privacy in and of itself. The problem is that we can't possibly anticipate all the ways that information might be used by companies whose motivations are completely different from ours as individuals. Facebook's invasion into my relationship was not the mere fact that it told lots of people about it. It crossed the line by deciding that our relationship news would be a good place to hang some ads, even though we didn't share the news ourselves. Seeing this sacred part of our life story used in that crass way was what pissed me off. These are the implications of the spiritual dimension of online privacy. If one doesn't want part of one's identity corrupted by such cynical, money-grubbing schemes, one shouldn't even let the ad-based web catch a whiff of it.

What might we lose, spiritually, when people get comfortable curating their private lives for public viewing, when our inner lives become public fodder? What are the spiritual implications when this becomes the new normal?

<<<< REWIRING OUR MINDS >>>>

Clearly, there's a balance to be struck between the power and convenience of technology and its harmful consequences and side effects. But it's not just a matter of deciding to use tech more carefully. Digital devices have worked their way into day-to-day life so thoroughly that they've changed our behavior in ways that we aren't even conscious of. Some of those ways are harmless, and maybe some are beneficial, but there's no question that some of our daily tech habits are deleterious, and we may not even be aware of the ways we've changed.

It's so easy to gather anecdotes to prove this. On a long walk through San Francisco with some friends, we stopped at a playground that had a neat, squishy surface made out of recycled shoes or something. A parent (or babysitter) was there with a little girl. The girl was up on the play structure chattering, singing, and climbing around. The grown up was standing next to it talking on the phone. Suddenly, the little girl turned, said "Catch me!" and then jumped off the structure toward the adult, who feebly raised one arm in self-defense. The child bounced off and landed on her bottom on the ground. This person proceeded to angrily interrupt her conversation to complain that the girl had jumped when she had "only had one freakin' arm to catch her with!" The adult's other arm, of course, was holding the phone.

This story is really not meant to shame anyone's parenting. Who am I to do that? I only tell it to bring attention to the words this person used to explain her frustration. "I only had one freakin' arm" is a bizarre way to think about the situation. The person had two arms, of course. It's just that the other one was holding a cell phone. This sentence and the frustration behind it seem to imply that the child should have known not to interrupt a grown up on a cell phone. Never mind the fact that these two human beings went to the playground together, which seems like a pretty reasonable place to play together!

The perspective that all this digital technology is just normal now is so comfortable that it's hard to shake, even though it has changed day-to-day life in such obviously absurd ways. Our behavior around smartphones is the stuff of stand-up comedy, things that seem reasonable to us in the situation, but which make our heads swirl with incomprehension when examined out of context. Regarding the killer epidemic of texting while driving, Louis C.K. says, "People are willing to risk taking a life and ruining their own because they don't want to be alone for a second."[4] We can't solve those problems with just more tech. We have to shift our perspective, too.

Yes, meditation practice is a great way to find perspective, though our tech and our practice can be tangled up in good ways, too. Recently, I was walking down the hill from my house listening to a podcast of a dharma talk. The talk was about the importance of embodied practice, being aware of the body as a source of truth and presence during meditation. The teacher said something particularly insightful about how easy it is to forget one's body, and suddenly, I realized I was disembodied! I was just floating down the hill listening and thinking, not feeling my feet on the pavement, not seeing the late afternoon sunlight through the trees. So I paused the lecture, took my earbuds out, and *BOOM*, the beauty of the present moment washed over me, and I basked in the feeling of authentic connection to the world.

The tech I had with me reminded me to turn it off because I had loaded it with a good reminder. Sure, it was distracting me before, but the distraction contained the seed of paying attention. That seemed like a profound lesson, so I took out my phone one more time, wrote down a reminder to write this chapter, and then put the phone back in my pocket and continued my walk.

<<<< SNAPPING OUT OF IT >>>>

I have learned other important lessons, sometimes the hard way, about the need to disconnect from the Internet and practice mindfulness as an integral part life. When I finally, deeply got the message, I had been writing about Internet companies and technologies full-time for about a year. I had all the latest gadgets and apps, all of them constantly buzzing with new information. I was on the West Coast of the U.S., in the heart of the tech bubble, but I had to wake up early enough to be on top of the East Coast's news, three time zones over. And I had to stay plugged in until the last of the Silicon Valley tech companies had switched over to the night shift.

During the day, my job was to pay attention to the industry in real time, watching multiple feeds of messages, announcements, breaking news, and new data. The second something important caught my eye, I had to drop what I was doing and write about it, pulling in enough background information to tell the whole story of the significance of this little byte of news, all while still trying to keep an eye out for more news. And this is what I was supposed to be doing *without* being interrupted by company meetings, inbound messages from PR people or sources, or friends and family (in descending order of priority).

In other words, I was just as busy as countless other busy, overstressed people. This is extremely commonplace for so-called "knowledge workers" (a term I hope expands to include one hundred percent of humanity before it poisons us all into thinking that working on a computer is a privilege for extra-knowledgeable people). That said, something about my situation felt particularly acute compared to my friends and peers in other lines of work. I was not only constantly plugged into the Internet; I was spending tons of time online talking, reading, and thinking *about* the Internet and the devices that connect to it. I was obligated to obsess over this constant connection and push it to its limits in order to understand it.

I began to see the negative side effects of this obsession in others first. Other tech journalists I knew seemed to be constantly distracted. I felt like I couldn't get to know them because a hefty portion of their attention was always directed elsewhere through their devices. And because their job was to be interested in that technology, they didn't seem to feel the least bit of compunction or conflict about it. Not on the surface, anyway.

The people I knew who actually work on tech products and services were slightly less crazed than the journalists, but that came with a corresponding narrowness of focus. They didn't have to be plugged in to everything that was happening, but they were seriously obsessed with the particular tech problems they worked on. I felt the same distance from them when I tried to connect one-on-one.

This awareness of the weirdness around plugged-in people grew alongside my own baseline stress levels as I continued to go about my business. But once I was sensitized to that weirdness, I started to see it more and more. I saw it all around me. No one looked up at anybody on the subway. Everyone at the café was sitting alone, typing. Little kids could be instantly pacified by parents handing them a $500 computer made of glass. It was like a *Twilight Zone* episode. Gradually but inevitably, I began to see myself behaving this way, too. I started to realize that the distance I was feeling from people in my life was not all on their side. Indeed, people who seemed totally present and rarely distracted when they were with me still felt distant. *It must be me*, I began to realize. *I'm only half-present.*

This realization brought back the words of my meditation teachers in college. I could remember the sentences, the logical statements about attending to the present moment and letting go of distracting thoughts, but I couldn't feel that they were true anymore. In college, I had a daily meditation practice. But during those years as a tech journalist, even when I gave myself the time to sit and meditate—which was rare—my brain just kept multitasking and jumping around, prewriting blog posts and tweets, thinking about the inner workings of tech companies, and otherwise continuing to work. This is an intimately familiar feeling to any meditator. It felt familiar to me. But I didn't have enough perspective to notice how much worse that mental noise was than when I had been meditating every day. Since then, I had retrained my brain in the opposite direction. I had established an anti-practice.

Unfortunately, I had to learn a tough lesson before I became aware of this enough to take action. One night, after a typically stressful day of work, I was unwinding on my bed, just lying on my back staring at the ceiling, trying to let my nerves cool down. That was a typical practice for me. After a day of news bombardment, my nervous system felt weirdly hot inside my body. I could actually feel the sensation. My roommate had a friend over, and they were talking loudly in the living room late into the night.

I should have simply gone into the room and asked them to be quiet. That was so obviously the responsible thing to do. But I was too burnt out. The simple act of standing up seemed impossible. More importantly, I was too divested from my in-person world that day to make the effort. I had been so deep down the rabbit hole in my online relationships that I thought of them before the people ten feet away from me.

So how did I deal with my irritation toward these people in my house, one of whom was a dear friend? I posted something snarky about them publicly online. It wasn't mean, exactly—at least my words weren't. But I had still done something mean. It contained identifying information about both of them, as well as their location. It violated their privacy. And as I should have expected, they saw it. I woke up the next morning to a hurt email from my roommate about it. I had made them feel violated and uncomfortable, all in the hopes of a cheap laugh from the Internet peanut gallery that I didn't even get.

I apologized immediately and deleted the post, but I still felt terrible. I walked to work the next day in this foggy mixture of emotional confusion and rational self-awareness. I saw what I had done, but I couldn't understand why I had done it. All I knew was that if I had controlled the impulse to post that message, if I had been more mindful of my relationship with my roommate and with myself, it wouldn't have happened. What was the nature of that compulsion to post? I quickly realized that I felt it constantly, almost every time I had a witty thought. It had just never troubled me before, because I hadn't caused any harm. Now that I had, it seemed important that I change my behavior somehow. But how could I? That behavior was my job and was also the norm all around me, for family and friends, strangers and neighbors, as well as colleagues. I was in the middle of a mass group think, so what might seem from the outside like total madness—like doctors and pregnant women chain-smoking in the 1950s—seemed completely ordinary.

When I tweeted that mean thing, part of me was acting deliberately. I had identified a snarky thing to say on Twitter at night, which was a formula that I saw work for others, and it had worked for me in the past. The emotional content of the tweet was just a stylistic thing from that vantage point. It didn't even occur to me (until it was too late) that the social consequences might outweigh the possible media benefits (pitiful though they would have been).

It sucks that being nice isn't the easiest possible course of action all the time. Stress upsets the equation, and clearly I was stressed out at the time. But there are a few more factors. I'm reminded of a popular college graduation speech given by the writer George Saunders in 2013. He points to this as "the million-dollar question: What's our problem? Why aren't we kinder?" His first two proposed reasons, while probably true for most people most of the time, remind me acutely of what it felt like to be a full-time blogger. "(1) We're central to the universe (that is, our personal story is the main and most interesting story, the only story, really); (2) we're separate from the universe (there's us and then, out there, all that other junk—dogs and swing-sets, and the state of Nebraska and low-hanging clouds and, you know, other people)."[5] The abstract feeling of spending most of my day disembodied, jockeying for attention in 2-D space surrounded by advertisements, overloaded me with that feeling. I *still* work mostly online—though in a much less intense way—and I can readily observe how much less I feel this way than I did then. This suggests to me that the more inundated by online media I am, the easier it is for me to feel solipsistic and uncaring.

In Zen stories, the moment of awakening often comes about in ridiculous ways. The monk gets slapped with a sandal, or the cook hocks a loogie on the floor, or something like that, and suddenly someone attains enlightenment. My first snap-out-of-it moment was caused by a tweet, but I wouldn't say I achieved sudden illumination. I had a sense that something was wrong and the Internet had something to do with it, but I didn't know quite what to say about it yet. I didn't know how to work it into my tech coverage, though it felt important for me to figure out a way.

< < < < THE DIGITAL DETOX > > > >

An answer came in a package that couldn't have been more perfectly wrapped. It turned out that worrying about these issues was getting trendy. Not long after the tweet incident, a friend of mine invited me along for a Digital Detox retreat he was about to attend. The Digital Detox is a Bay Area-based start-up. It puts on offline retreats and events for tech-addled people. They're expensive and comfortable, not exactly monastic experiences, but they're rustic and nature-centered, and they do have a fairly serious introspective and therapeutic, even generally spiritual component. I couldn't tell which part made me more excited: the opportunity to go completely offline for four days, or the great tech story I would get out of it.

I paid my own way, but my editors let me go off the grid for the better part of a week to get the story. We turned off our phones the second we got in the car. I did so joyously, knowing that, in this rare instance, there was no professional reason I had to be online, and I could completely relax about it. That feeling only intensified when we reached the remote hot springs where the retreat was held. And when we met the Digital Detox founders, Levi and Brooke, and the other guests, all thought of the world outside the retreat melted away.

The group of people on a retreat like that is self-selecting, and there was an instant affinity among us. I'm not sure if it would still be this way now that retreats explicitly about getting away from digital technology have become more fashionable, but in 2012 it was still a somewhat exotic idea. The first dinner brought us together immediately as we went around the table and shared our reasons for being there.

All of us took very seriously the need to be completely separated from the digital parts of our lives. Even discussing them at that initial dinner felt stressful. We quickly realized we needed a rule not to talk about work. We began calling it "the W-word." But reading between the lines, it was clear that many of the people on the retreat worked in high-tech jobs. They were as freaked out by professional-grade Internet use as I was.

Techies comprised roughly two-thirds of the group, and I may have been the most extreme case of technology addiction, but none of the techies were far behind. The other third was different, though. While we were all there for the same basic reason, a retreat from high technology, there was a clear divide in underlying motivations.

The techies were there because their lives were flooded with online interactions. It was a necessary condition for them most of the time. Many of them enjoyed the fast pace of that life; they just realized they needed a break to recharge.

The other third, however, was always wary of technology. Some of them didn't even use computers in their jobs. But what little computer use was required of them overwhelmed them, and they struggled to resist the social pressure all around them to be online. For them, this retreat was a refuge. At last, they could get away from the demands of a world that seemed to insist they change their innermost nature in order to adapt.

The difference between these two groups would prove to be the real challenge of the retreat. Over the next three days, as we meditated and did yoga, hiked in the woods, made art, and ate healthy, mindful meals, I think most of us experienced flashes of fear of missing out on what was happening back on the grid, but those all passed quickly. It wasn't a big deal. Being offline felt good, but there were things we missed. Not surprising. The real challenge was understanding why we needed this retreat. We needed to understand that, in order to learn how to adjust our normal lives to make us happier.

The last exercise of the retreat was a conversation about how to return to the world. It was the first time we talked about life back on the grid since the opening dinner, in which we had decided "work" was a profane word. After being on the same page all weekend, when all we had to do was sink into the feeling of disconnection, we started disagreeing with each other almost immediately as the closing conversation began.

People on the high-tech side of the spectrum started coming up with strategies for reintegrating into the frenetic pace of their work lives, seeking each other's help in getting ready to return. The low-tech people began wondering, *Why not just stay like this? Why go back to that way of life at all?* The high-tech people began to feel attacked. *Because that's our job, that's our way of life. We need a better way to cope. That's why we came on this retreat.* But, the low-tech people argued, constant connectivity is clearly harmful and unhealthy. That's why we all felt so good all weekend on this disconnected retreat. *You're just going to go back to your unhealthy ways now?*

The discussion became heated, and there was no resolution. Eventually, the leaders of the retreat had to cut us off and make us go outside in the sunshine. That made us happy again, at least, but I left the retreat without a clear sense of what I had gained, other than nice memories of a relaxing weekend with a great group.

While I certainly felt that a few days off the grid doing yoga and eating healthily was good for the body and mind, those just seemed like luxuries. That was fine for a group mostly comprised of California tech people, but it was hardly radical. It didn't break from the dominant ideology that got us there. If anything, it supported it. Now that we were "recharged"—just like phones—we could go back into the world at full power. I don't think that's how the leaders of the retreat positioned it, and some of the participants were certainly not thinking of themselves as recharged phones. But a refreshing return to high-tech life was an inevitable result for most of us, myself included. So I went back to my tech job and wrote the Digital Detox story. Then I kept writing occasional little posts about the issue of disconnection, because it kept popping up in my mind. It was as if something had snapped inside of me. An isolated retreat was not good enough. I couldn't stop noticing the negative side effects of the high-tech life I was living. Business as usual wouldn't work for me anymore. The transformation was underway.

Disconnection is clearly good for the soul. But occasional, isolated retreats aren't enough to preserve the benefits of it. We need some time offline every day. It quiets down our minds, it tunes us in to our immediate surroundings, and it manages the expectation that we're always available to others. "The joy of non-doing is that nothing else needs to happen for this moment to be complete," writes Jon Kabat-Zinn in *Wherever You Go, There You Are*.[6] "Perhaps such moments of non-doing are the greatest gift one can give oneself."

We can also engage with the world in that state, without the Internet, as we always have. Time online can improve and increase our engagement with society, science, religion, and our friends, and those benefits are worth the risks as long as we practice balance. But that balance has to be part of a spiritual mission. Putting down the phone is not the end goal. It's just the beginning. It's one principle among many.

Once I started thinking this way, I knew I had to expand the scope of my work beyond tech for tech's sake. I thought about Burning Man, a Bay Area–based counterculture that builds a week-long art-city in the Black Rock Desert of Nevada each summer, which had been my spiritual home for years. Alongside my work covering technology, I had been volunteering as a blogger on the Burning Man website. My day job also let me write one post about Burning Man each year. I made the case to them that it was an important part of Silicon Valley culture, and that its social norms about technology were interesting enough to merit a story. But after the Digital Detox shook me up, I saw it as something more than that. I saw it as my yearly rite of passage out of the frantic time of high-tech society and into the deep, natural time that shapes who we are.

All spiritual seekers have ways of making this passage. Perhaps yours is your meditation practice. Perhaps it's organized religion or some radically personal spirituality. Maybe it's art, music, or dance. Maybe it's gardening or kayaking or some other kind of wilderness connection. Maybe it's all of these things. One of mine is my annual pilgrimage to Burning Man. Burning Man is not for everyone. Lots of deeply spiritual, cool people I know think Burning Man is totally lame. Honestly, I think so too on occasion. But it has taught me so much about living a mindful, balanced life in community. It was one of my gateways into a lifelong spiritual practice. Come through that gate with me for a little while. I'll take you on my personal tour of that ephemeral desert city. You don't have to stay long. Then we'll come back to the default world—as the old-school Burners call mainstream society—and bring with us some principles and practices for being present and mindful, even in a dazzlingly high-tech world.

<<<< THE PRINCIPLES OF BURNING MAN >>>>

Did you know that the first-ever Google Doodle in 1998 was the Burning Man logo? The cofounders of Google, Larry Page and Sergey Brin, were serious Burners, and they needed a way to indicate to the tiny handful of Google (then known as Google!) users in 1998 that they were away that week and couldn't fix any problems. So they put the Burning Man logo into the second O of Google(!), closed up shop, and went to the desert, and that's where Google's tradition of decorating the logo on their home page began.

The first time I visited the Google campus was in 2011, when I started covering the company for work. I knew this story about the Google Doodle, but I still didn't expect to see photos of Burning Man all over the walls of the lobbies of Building 43. Every official encounter I had with Google from that point on bore the mark of Burning Man. They had robotic art from the festival fully wired up at their parties. Probably half of the Googlers I interviewed had been to Burning Man multiple times. One day, leaving an interview at Google for the drive back up to Oakland, I saw big, metal shark fins permanently installed in the center of campus. I had leaned against one of those very fins to watch the Man burn for the first time.

That first Burn was in 2008. Five friends and I had flown across the country from Boston to Oakland with duffel bags crammed full of neon clothes. The plan was to drive north to Mendocino County, where one of my friends had grown up, to prepare and pack up in the woods for a couple days. The people we were camping with lived up there, and we could all drive out to Nevada together. As soon as we landed, and as we drove up the Northern California coastline into the night, I could already feel my life changing.

I had first heard about Burning Man when I was in fourth grade, growing up in Atlanta. My teacher, Peter Richards, told us a story about his son, Austin. On the playa—the flat, dried-up, prehistoric lakebed in Nevada where the event is held—Austin's name is Dr. Megavolt. Peter told us that Dr. Megavolt performed lightning shows at a place called Burning Man. I don't think Peter quite knew how to explain the workings of a Tesla coil to a room full of fourth graders, but we got the picture. Dr. Megavolt dressed up like a robot, waved a magic wand in the air, and a giant metal tower shot lightning bolts at him while people watched and cheered. That was a sufficient explanation of what "Burning Man" meant to me. It didn't occur to me for a long time that Burning Man was an actual place where Dr. Megavolt wouldn't even be the center of attention that night.

The next time I heard the words "Burning Man" was my senior year of high school. My friends and I were looking for something to do one weekend, and we heard about an event called Ripe that was being held all night in some empty lot on the west side of Atlanta. Whoever told us about Ripe mentioned two other facts about it: it was all-ages, and it was an "unofficial Burning Man event." We all had a vague sense of what Burning Man was about—this was 2005, after Burning Man's creep into pop culture awareness was underway—so we knew it would be cooler than anything a bunch of high school seniors could come up with themselves. We didn't understand what Ripe's relationship to the desert festival was, but we figured the association was a good sign. So we put on some hippie clothes and drove out there.

Ripe was not what we expected. It was so much more... innocent. There were kids running around all over the place, playing on the art. There were no obviously drunk people. It was a pretty serene atmosphere, actually. There were a few little lean-to structures with black lights and puff-painted art inside. They were circled around a big, rusty, metal sculpture with a roaring fire inside, which was the main source of light in this vacant lot. Some light electronic music was piped in over a speaker system, and people joined in with little flutes and drums. There were performers spinning fire *poi*, which was something I'd never seen before. And everyone was smiling and talking to strangers and generally enjoying each other. The rest of our friends were probably shouting at each other over the music at some house party, but we found ourselves quite pleased with this mellow scene.

We had instinctively brought one activity to do together. We had a big pad of newsprint paper with sticky stuff on the back and a bag full of markers. We spread out the pad and markers on the ground and started drawing and writing artsy, stream-of-consciousness stuff from all angles on the paper. The collaborative part was what made it interesting. Our writings and drawings would react to and join on to each other. This turned out to be an excellent way to meet people. People would wander over on their own, or we'd beckon them over, and we'd all work on one together. Then we'd tear it off and stick it up on a Porta-Potty door or a telephone pole, and that was our contribution to the art at Ripe. Many years of Burning Man later, I still admire how close we came to the Burner ethos without even knowing it. We missed one key part, though: to be good Burners, we should have collected all our art at the end and packed it out. Or thrown it on the fire.

Three short years after Ripe, I hit the playa for the first time. We were still miles from the gate when I realized how much huger and louder Burning Man was going to be than Ripe had led me to expect, and I knew I was psychologically underprepared. It was the middle of the night on Sunday. The week-long festival had barely even started yet, and the doors and windows of our car were already vibrating from the thumping dance music. We could see glowing towers belching fire and spewing lasers, and they were *miles* away from us. This couldn't be accurately described as a party. This was a city.

Yet I could still somehow see the cultural association with that little party in an Atlanta parking lot. There was something tangibly twenty-first-century about it. All around us, people were pouring out of their waiting vehicles and dancing on the dusty Gate Road. They represented a kind of diversity I'd never seen. It wasn't the broad diversity of history and perspective that I was used to from growing up in a big city. These people all had something in common, some kind of openness and drive and curiosity I couldn't put my finger on yet. Some of them were eighteen and some of them were seventy. Some of them were speaking Australian-accented English and some were speaking Japanese. Some were wearing gas masks and trench coats, some nothing but paint and funny hats. And this was just in the line to get inside!

As I biked around the dusty streets of Black Rock City that week, I came to a clearer understanding of what made all these crazy people seem so familiar after a while. There were some underlying principles at work, magic words flying around that changed the way people treated each other there. People I met kept talking about Immediacy and Radical Self-Reliance and Participation, terms I could understand immediately because I saw them happening all around me. Even Decommodification, which was clearly a made-up word, made sense when I saw how people had blocked out the brand names of their rental trailers and shade structures with black tape. Eventually, I started inquiring into the origin of these terms, and everyone I talked to about it knew some version of the story.

Over twenty-five years or so, Burning Man had grown from an informal gathering on a beach in San Francisco to a big, informal gathering in the Black Rock Desert and then to a 60,000-person, carefully organized temporary city (of tents, cars, robot dragon-ducks, and chaos and disorder). Eventually, the organizers realized they had a culture on their hands. The event was growing and changing under its own power, so they couldn't exert force and control what it would be. And its influence was spreading out into the wider world, spawning regional events like Ripe and changing people's work and relationships and goals in life. There was a movement happening, and it needed to coordinate its efforts and language. People began to write into the Burning Man office asking for some kind of understandable, consistent message they could share to explain what this culture was about. So Larry Harvey and other founding Burners started to do some ethnographic work on their own participants to figure out what their values were. The list he came up with became known as the Ten Principles.

To be clear, these principles were not imposed on the event. They were distilled from the words and deeds of the longtime participants who make Burning Man what it is. But as the event grew and became a pop culture phenomenon, the number of new participants skyrocketed. First-time Burners quickly swelled to some 40 percent of Black Rock City's population, and regional activities across the globe introduced vastly more people to Burning Man culture. The Ten Principles needed names for educational reasons. It formalized the values that made Burning Man what it is, and it made them teachable.

These principles are Radical Inclusion, Gifting, Decommodification, Radical Self-Reliance, Radical Self-Expression, Communal Effort, Civic Responsibility, Leaving No Trace, Participation, and Immediacy. Most of them are quite easy to explain.

Radical Inclusion means everyone is welcome and involved.

Gifting is the mode of transaction in Burner culture; you don't buy and sell or trade—you just give and receive gifts.

Decommodification means no brands or advertising, which makes everything more sacred.

Radical Self-Reliance means take care of yourself out there in the desert.

Radical Self-Expression means you get to be the most you there is.

Communal Effort means work together to make this whole thing possible.

Civic Responsibility means take care of each other and the city.

Leaving No Trace means leave the playa exactly as you found it, and pack out every single molecule of trash.

Participation means you are not a spectator! You're in the show!

Immediacy, the last principle and my personal favorite, means always remain in the present moment.

Nobody's perfect, but I've always been amazed by how closely people hew to these principles at Burning Man. I can't believe it works, but it does. These values hold the community together out there.

One interesting thing about the Ten Principles is that they often contradict each other. "Sometimes the exception to a rule can deepen understanding of a principle," Larry Harvey writes in the Ten Principles Blog Series, which began in 2013 as a way to officially deepen the meaning and historical importance of the principles.[7]

"If, for example, Radical Self-Reliance is held to imply unaided survivalism, how can it possibly correspond to Communal Effort? Philosophy occurs when principles collide, and we should allow these Principles to interpret and interrogate one another."[8]

I think it's actually this dialog between the principles that makes it possible for Burners to wield them. You can get into some weird situations at Burning Man. You may find yourself standing alone in the dark when a giant, glowing rainbow fish pulls up blasting disco music, rocking back and forth as people dance all over it. It came out of nowhere and stopped right in front of you. In that absurd situation, you have a decision to make: Are you feeling Radical Self-Reliance out there alone? Is that what you want to explore? Or do you feel the call of Participation? Do you want to go into the light and dance? You know the people onboard will welcome you with Radical Inclusion if you do. This is the way the crisscrossing principles work as signposts for deciding how to be moment by moment, even when things get strange.

Inevitably, you end up taking these values home with you. After spending one week—or one week a year—in a society that functions on these principles, you don't want to stop. That's why Burning Man culture inevitably spread into a year-round, worldwide phenomenon. What I didn't know at the time was that Ripe was a tiny party by the standards of Burning Man regional events. Afrika-Burn, the official regional event in South Africa had more than 10,000 participants in 2014. That's the size Burning Man was the year after it was on the cover of *Wired* magazine. Regional events happen all year long. But Burner culture thrives back home in the cities of those regions, too. In San Francisco, people who don't go to Burning Man celebrate that one week in late August when they can find parking anywhere in the city. For the rest of the year, Burning Man participants have a huge influence on the culture of the place, and that's increasingly true in places like Melbourne and Tel Aviv and especially Reno, Nevada, the nearest big city to the Burning Man event.

As I kept going back to Burning Man over the years, I kept exploring and writing about its culture. I was fascinated by the way that this temporary desert city seemed to have fixed something about modern life. It was one thing when I saw the thousands of paying participants treating each other well. But then I saw the way the values translated into the real world, and that's when I really started to believe. I saw initiatives like Burners Without Borders—an organization that sends Burners, with their estimable skills at building a habitat in challenging conditions—into international disaster areas to help rebuild; and Black Rock Solar, which is making serious headway in renewable energy; not to mention all the grants provided to artists around the world. Burning Man values seemed to instill a real desire in people to build a better future.

That's around the time I started writing about tech full time, and I began to learn that companies like Google were founded by Burners and had art and photos up all over campus. It made sense to me when I thought about Google's company culture. They certainly seemed to value breaking rules, being creative, and trying to improve the future. They're doing that at all costs. After a while, it began to freak me out a little bit. It became clear that massively wealthy, insular tech people made up a surprisingly large chunk of the Burning Man population.

Part of me wanted to resent that—it felt like mixing work and play for me—but the issue was too complicated for a simple stance. Those same people were building some of the most ambitious and powerful stuff on the playa. Some Burning Man art is purely ostentatious, sure, but some installations are so inventive, requiring whole new programming languages or 3-D-printed pieces just to build them. Clearly, people whose day jobs were inventing the miraculous-yet-ominous consumer technologies all around us must be incredibly creative people. Burning Man was where they got to unplug and let loose. I was glad they took the chance, because Burning Man is not for everyone. It's hard to live in that desert for a week, bringing everything you need along with you. I began to respect the tech people who went to Burning Man for it.

As the influence of tech on Burning Man became clear to me, it also became a pretty good story to write about. I wrote about it for the tech site for a few years, but as I became more and more of a Burner, the dark side of my closeness to the Ten Prnciples began to catch up with me too. That principle of Immediacy kept coming up. Whenever I was on my phone, I was ignoring the Immediacy of my surroundings. That's why the principle works so well at Burning Man; there's no phone service out there! That doesn't stop techie Burners from trying, of course. There are plenty of camps with Wi-Fi. That's fine. Radical Inclusion, right? It takes all kinds. But for me, I began to see that tech had its place, but it wasn't healthy for me to have it as my main focus. I still couldn't shake the feeling that there was something just a little bit incongruous happening. The presence of the tech industry at Burning Man made sense on some level, but it felt a little eerie.

I'm far from alone in that observation. In the *London Review of Books* in July 2014, Emily Witt published a Burning Man diary that rang pretty true for me (and I read a *LOT* of such things). At the end, she described the burning of a pyramid topped with a giant icon of the Facebook Like button in 2013, a burn which I watched from up close with absolute glee.

> No wonder people hate Burning Man, I thought,
> when I pictured it as a cynic might: rich people
> on vacation breaking rules that everyone else
> would be made to suffer for not obeying. Many
> of these people would go back to their lives and
> back to work on the great farces of our age.
> They wouldn't argue for the decriminalisation
> of the drugs they had used; they wouldn't want
> anyone to know about their time in the orgy
> dome. That they had cheered at the funeral
> pyre of a Facebook "like" wouldn't play well on
> Tuesday in the cafeteria at Facebook. The peo-
> ple who accumulated the surplus value of the
> world's photographs, 'life events' and ex-boy-
> friend obsessions were now celebrating their
> freedom from the web they'd entangled all of us
> in, the freedom to exist without the internet.[9]

That's all very true. Lots of Burners just go back to their
routines and hide what it was like from the rest of the
world. There's no way a Burner who took Burner culture
seriously could go back and work on making the Like
button more addictive, but many do. Therefore, as many
outsiders see it, Burning Man is hypocritical. While we're

at it, how can people who call themselves environmentalists drive across the land with 60,000 people and start burning giant wooden statues every year? These criticisms, like the contradictions between the Ten Principles, are exactly what make Burning Man such an interesting subject to write about. After all, it's not as if people do a great job of living up to their highest ethical principles elsewhere in the world. What is it about the Burning Man experiment that makes these high-minded principles work even *some* of the time?

That question is the reason I still go to Burning Man. That's the reason I've managed—after years of earnestly trying—to find gainful work writing about the event and its culture for the Burning Man Project. This culture, even just considered as an ideal, seems like a good example to follow for a better life. The world is overwhelming and exciting and full of fire-breathing dragons and robots and blinking lights. It doesn't function without Participation. It doesn't hold together without Civic Responsibility and Communal Effort. It's not sustainable unless we work on Leaving No Trace. And if we don't practice Immediacy, we miss out on our very lives.

SPIRITUAL PRACTICES

< < < < THE SABBATH > > > >

At the end of the first week of the biblical universe, the Creator rested and beheld the new Creation. In doing so, the Creator created a pattern for all life to follow, to keep the Sabbath and experience its spiritual rejuvenation, refraining from all work for a day. Whether you're into the Bible or couldn't care less, this Sabbath thing probably seems like a good idea. Feel free to use your own language. Call it the weekend. Call it going on retreat. I call it Shabbat, a Hebrew word related to the verb *lashevet*, to sit (how about that, Buddhists?), rendered in English as the Sabbath.

In his beautiful book *The Sabbath*, Rabbi Abraham Joshua Heschel taught that the Day of Rest is like a "great cathedral" of time. It's our opportunity to shift away from a working week made of space and the material things that occupy it. The Sabbath is a palace made of time, with the sunsets on either side forming luminous walls. For an entire day, we can wrap ourselves in the blanketing expanse of the day itself, occupying time instead of space.

"Time is like a wasteland," Rabbi Heschel says. "It has grandeur but no beauty. Its strange, frightful power is always feared but rarely cheered. Then we arrive at the seventh day, and the Sabbath is endowed with a felicity, which enraptures the soul, which glides into our thoughts with a healing sympathy. It is a day on which hours do not oust one another."[1] Doesn't that just sound delicious?

Digital technology has radically transformed our sense of time. Analog time lengthens and shortens with the passing of the seasons. It moves in cycles that progress gradually and overlap. The progression of the sun and moon, the tides, the seasons, the years, the progressions of the planets and stars across the sky, the tectonic and geological shifting of the Earth—these are the background of time against which analog life evolved. Now life has its own cycles of time, its growth and decay, its metabolisms and circadian rhythms and gestation periods, and lately, its perception and cognition of change. All of that is the time in which we really live.

The digital imposition of fixed units of time is at

odds with natural time. It has imposed a sense of order on life. Human beings have used that order to organize an amazing civilization. But trying to live in that digital time, in spite of our brains and bodies, makes us uncomfortable, anxious, even unhealthy. We give up sleep our body needs for the sake of made-up digital time! It's just what we have to do to get by sometimes. But that doesn't mean it's good for us.

We're taught by physicists that space and time are really a continuum: space-time. But subjectively, we rarely experience the whole continuum at once. Space and time feel like discrete modes of being to us. That's why we have two different words for them. But maybe the words created the modes. Maybe there is no discreteness to space and time outside of our conceptual frame. It's hard to say. Maybe our answer changes over time. Sometimes we need an answer. At other times, let it change. In the world of space, of things, we wrestle for answers. On Shabbat, we can let go of the things and let time do its work.

Sliding even deeper into the mystical, we hear that time is an illusion anyway. In the deepest reality, everything is unified, all is change; it's only our mental illusions that impose a sense of linearity, of time passing. Maybe that's true, maybe not. Maybe it's nonsense; maybe the truth is nonsense. Time has many apparent, counterintuitive natures to us. The relentless march of seconds on a digital clock is not a sufficient picture of reality.

Some of my favorite understandings of time are from a short, beautiful novel called *Einstein's Dreams* by MIT physicist Alan Lightman. Each chapter is a description of a world with radically different characteristics of time as observed from Berne, Switzerland, at dawn in the spring of 1905. As a young Albert Einstein toils to finish his special theory of relativity, he dreams of these alternate worlds where time moves backward, forward, or randomly, or it doesn't move, or all of human life takes place in one day. Lightman describes what life would be like in these fantastical worlds of strange time, and the striking thing about it is that the subjective part of each description feels a little bit true.

The story from "29 May 1905" is one of the deepest to me, in that it merely exaggerates a truth of physics that Einstein was trying to elucidate for the first time, that "time passes more slowly for people in motion" than for people at rest. This effect is only measurable at speeds close to the speed of light, of course, but that doesn't make the observation at the end of the story any less poignant: "Some argue that only the giant clock tower on Kramgasse keeps the true time, that it alone is at rest. Others point out that even the giant clock is in motion when viewed from the river Aare, or from a cloud."[2] Every object exists in a truly different time, it's just that the differences are too slight for us to notice most of the time.

It's fun to contrast the time poetry of a physicist with mind-bending Buddhist descriptions of time, such as those from Dōgen, founder of the Sōtō school of Zen. The *Uji* fascicle of his seminal (and difficult to comprehend) *Shōbōgenzō* is full of awesome time riddles. "Just reflect," he implores us, "right now, is there an entire being or an entire world missing from your present time, or not?" There isn't, if you think about it. But don't think about it too much. "You should not come to understand that time is only flying past," Dōgen teaches. "You should not only learn that flying past is the virtue inherent in time. If time were to give itself to merely flying past, it would have to leave gaps." That is, as translators Norman Waddell and Masao Abe mercifully explain, "If time were merely flying past, there would be no unifying principle of the present, and thus 'gaps' everywhere."[3]

Time is always changing, passing differently for every object everywhere. Yet it is also always present, unchanging, here and constant, without gaps. Both of these ideas are true at once. The nature of time apparently depends on one's perspective. Shabbat institutes a change in perspective that results in a different nature of time. Meditation practice does this as well. According to our new understanding of technology, these are technologies for manipulating time.

By entering the cathedral of time, we make time invaluable. During the week, we may wish away time by yearning for the end of the day, the end of the week, the end of the semester, the end of the meeting. We may feel that time is scarce, wishing we could buy more, so we wouldn't feel so rushed. We may swing wildly between those values of time all day, because the value of time is relative to the space around us and the things and conditions in front of us. On the Sabbath, every moment is equally precious. Not just the present moment, but every infinitely small, infinitely big moment of the Sabbath is precious, because it's our whole day of rest.

If you have a daily mindfulness practice, perhaps you're smiling at this, because meditation teachers instruct us to focus on the present moment. But the lesson is the same: every moment, infinitely big, infinitely small, is precious because it's *right now*, which is all there is.

Usually, our worldly routines still sweep us away, and that's understandable. That's what Shabbat is for. That's what meditation is for. These sacred periods create time for rest from the torrential downpour of time in action. To be clear, rest is not idleness. If you're totally inert, there's no need for rest. Rest is recovery from action. Action in the world is where we give our life meaning. Rest gives us time to appreciate our lives of action, understand that meaning, and restore our energy, so we can go back for more. Later. After Shabbat.

Without rest, we break down. Our bodies insist on resting every night, so they can restore themselves for another day of action. What a clever technology sleep is. But we also benefit from resting our waking selves. It restores the dreamlike quality of living to our waking surroundings, our homes and meals and friends, making the mundane holy again. Most importantly, unlike the inner world of dreams, the Sabbath lets us rest with each other in the outer world we share.

The effect of the Sabbath on relationships is key. During the working week, we may treat our relationships as things, as instrumental to what needs to be done: the work, the chores, the cooking and cleaning. Sharing the workload is how humans survive. That's precisely why the social realm is so important to us. But on the Sabbath, when we do no work, there's a great pause, and those relationships are relieved of the mutual need. There's just another being there, smiling at you, needing nothing. And you need nothing from that being. Not even the smile. But you get the smile anyway, which makes you smile back.

The Sabbath is not just a time travel technology. It's

also good for healing relationships that are worn down by the needs of work. It's an opportunity to develop stronger ties. It's a platform. A social networking platform. Yes! I said that! I used Silicon Valley buzzwords to describe the Sabbath! Maybe you're as grossed out right now as I was when I wrote this paragraph. But I'm getting to the end of it now, and I already see the opportunity for healing. The problem is not putting Shabbat in the same category as Facebook. The problem is Facebook trying to play in the same category as Shabbat!

Facebook, which I'm using as a brand-name stand-in for all products of its kind—just as I am with Shabbat— is designed around need-based relationships. At least it is at the time of this writing. Maybe a few editions of this book from now, things will have changed. That's not a problem per se. The problem is that it positions itself as both a tool and a place for all relationships and all aspects of them at all times. Its interface and its notifications are the same on Shabbat as they are on Tuesday.

For Jews, there are plenty of concrete, religious proscriptions against using computers on Shabbat, and the distracting, needy interfaces of social media are just a period at the end of the sentence. Real-time, ad-supported social media were not a spiritual problem the rabbis anticipated. But I think we've covered plenty of additional questions they raise about the way we mediate our relationships through technology and our relationship with technology itself. It's pretty easy to make the case that regular, extended breaks from social media are necessary for the soul.

Now I think we've gotten to the heart of that idea. The spiritual challenge of being constantly connected to the pounding pulse of the Internet is that instrumental sense of always needing others and being needed for something. That digital pulse pulls us out of time and into space. Every text message is a need. Every selfie is a need. Those needs interrupt our flow of time, insisting they be met right now. The Sabbath is our chance to rest, to put down the weight of need, and to feel the relief of sitting in a cathedral of time.

The regular reminder of the Sabbath calls us back to an appreciation of the spaciousness of time. It calls us back to the key question of this inquiry into the spiritual relationship with technology: *What are you doing with your time right now?*

<<<< MANAGING INSIDE AND OUT >>>>

You can't rest all the time. You've got jobs to do. You're probably all too aware of some of them. Others are things you won't realize need doing until you're right in the middle of them. But as always, in that classically human combination of knowing what you're doing and winging it, you'll muddle through. It'll all get done eventually. Somehow.

We're lucky we have all these technologies at our disposal to help out. The companies that make them are quick to remind us of that, too. They want to be sure we know they're there for us. Every so often, they'll send us a little buzz just to remind us. If we forget about them for too long, maybe they'll send us an email. "We haven't seen you around lately. Is everything okay? Your friends miss you! Come back and tell them what you've been up to!"

That's where they get you, keeping up with your friends. Web and mobile technologies are increasingly designed around this model of constant social interaction. While you're away from those technologies, it seems everybody else is still buzzing away, making things, getting recognition, having the best time.

Pundits coined this term "FOMO"—Fear Of Missing Out—to describe that nagging feeling that you're supposed to be *there*, wherever *there* is, just because your social tech makes you feel that way. FOMO has spawned a whole cottage industry of people fighting back against this perceived threat with calls to disconnect, to detox from the tech addiction and try to impose some change in the culture to keep us from feeling this way. Maybe you even thought you were reading that kind of book right now.

But no, I wouldn't give so much power to the

technology itself. *We* hired *it*, remember? Not the other way around. We just have to be better managers. We have to make sure the technology is doing the job we hired it for, and we especially have to ensure that it isn't doing other jobs we *don't* want done.

The trick is, we have to be able to manage ourselves first. The only reason tech can get to us, no matter how deviously it is designed, is that we are prone to the distraction it offers. Mindfulness practice is a proven technology for strengthening us against interruptions and distractions, as well as strengthening our positive resolve to listen, to be present to our needs and the needs of others, and to concentrate on what truly matters. Once we have the strength and flexibility gained through mindfulness training, we are much better equipped to handle the wily nature of personal tech and use its volatile powers for good.

Our tech can get into all kinds of trouble, and when it does, it drags us into it. It takes on jobs we never intended to give it, like nagging us about what our friends are doing until we get FOMO, for instance. It's a problem of capacity. Computers are getting so fast that they have plenty of spare time after they're done doing the jobs we gave them on purpose. Now they can just run in the background waiting for the notifications to come in. Meanwhile, the capacity of *our minds* to handle information is being pushed to the limit. We get overwhelmed by data much more quickly than computers do, and computers lack the empathy (so far) to see that. If we tell the computer to help us by giving us information, it will help us into oblivion if we let it.

Unfortunately, so often, we do let this happen. External demands and internal impulses weigh on us and convince us to slip, and then we start letting the jobs creep up beyond what we intended initially because, hey, we can squeeze it in. I've got five people ahead of me in line. Let's play a game. I'm sitting here reading a book, but why don't I just pop over to this other app for a second and see if anything fun is going on tonight?

These don't sound like jobs deserving of the name, but try thinking about them that way. If we want the job done of letting us play a game while we're in line, we hire a smartphone and an app to do it. It sounds weird, but the analogy works the more you run with it. It works the other way, too. Regular jobby-jobs, as in work jobs, can get off track with the same kinds of distractions. Any project, even an entire person's job, can bloat up to fill all the space it's given instead of staying tightly focused on the mission. We call that mission creep. It starts with good intentions, wanting to accomplish all kinds of things, but it ends up overloading us and running us off the rails.

The solution to this problem is not to fire everybody, though. It's to be a better manager. You're the manager of yourself, so you'll need a strong mindfulness practice for that job. And you're the manager of the technology you've hired to do various other jobs. So if you find yourself getting easily distracted on your computer or phone, are you going to throw the device away? If you're distracted by browsing the web while you're at work, should you just shut your laptop and go outside instead of finishing what you're working on? No, you can't do that. You just have to manage better. That means practicing mindfulness to weaken the pull of distraction from inside, as well as reducing the distractions coming at you from outside.

It's important to remember that it's in the thick of our daily work that spiritual practice matters most. That's why we call it practice. It's all well and good if we can focus while sitting on a cushion silently with our eyes closed, but only if that makes us better at focusing while we're in a stressful day-to-day situation.

When we're really present to what that's like, we realize that it can make mundane and everyday situations, even the unpleasant ones, into powerfully illuminating experiences. There's a reason Zen monks are so fastidious about sweeping the floor. And there's no reason that using your computers can't be like that. Checking email is just like sweeping the floor, whether you find it terrible or liberating. The dust—or the email—keeps piling up, and we keep sweeping it away. That's the stuff of everyday life, and as all the great teachers teach us, it's the heart of the practice. "I can lose myself and find myself simultaneously while cleaning the kitchen stove," says Jon Kabat-Zinn.[4] If your goal is liberation, if your work is spiritual work, then you can make your technology—whether it's a broom or a phone—an instrument of liberation.

<<<< THE TECHNOLOGY OF MEDITATION >>>>

The Buddhists teach—and it's easy to agree—that living a skillful life begins by paying attention. Paying attention is difficult, and we often stray, doing things carelessly or by accident. But with focus, we can apply ourselves more consistently. In combination with clear goals and firm values, paying attention is what keeps us on the right path. As Omori Sogen teaches in *An Introduction to Zen Training*, "Just as you focus on a target before you aim an arrow, if you focus your mind and decisively determine the direction in which you are going, you are already halfway there."[5]

So getting better at our life's work is not just a matter of practicing its particular skills. We also have to practice this fundamental skill of paying attention, which will in turn improve the quality of our other practices.

How do we get better at paying attention? Ultimately, the best attention practice anyone has found is meditation, the persistent redirecting of attention back to the present moment.

But there are myriad ways we can make our meditation practice harder or easier for ourselves. We make it harder by surrounding ourselves with distractions, by juggling many concerns in our heads, by building a routine that's full of interruptions, not making enough time for meditation, and even intentionally escaping what's true in the present by indulging in fantasies that are more entertaining. But we can make it easier for ourselves by planning our time well, by reducing distractions, and by keeping our minds clear to focus on the important things. And that is where technology can help us.

Meditation itself is a technology. It's an elegant tool we've developed for working with the capabilities and limitations of our own brains and minds as they are. But our external information technologies can give us an enormous boost in managing our attention and focusing on the present. Even the most mundane technique of technological attention management is performing a sacred, meditative function. It helps us concentrate on our practice of mindfulness, and in turn it improves our work.

This seems counterintuitive at first. Technology seems to provide the ultimate distraction. Television and the Internet provide endless wells of novelty, and mobile devices bring that constant newness insistently into our pockets, buzzing us unendingly. Tech doesn't merely seem like a difficult match with a mindful lifestyle, it seems like the complete antithesis of mindfulness.

But the benefits of technology are all in what you use it for and how you use it. Even meditation is not exempt from the pitfalls of technology. So much of the beginning of the contemplative path is spent avoiding pitfalls. Teachers warn of flawed but easily understandable motivations in novice practitioners that could derail the whole project of meditative training. "The path of truth is profound—and so are the obstacles and possibilities for self-deception," Chögyam Trungpa Rinpoche warns in *Cutting through Spiritual Materialis*m.[6] If one's motivation to meditate is the ambition to attain exalted states of consciousness, access exclusive wisdom, be revered by others, or any other selfish interest driven by attachment or craving, one will make little or no progress or even move backwards, learning bad habits and letting them settle in.

Similarly, technologies capable of clearing out distractions and facilitating focus can also derail their users and cause a breakdown of attention. The most classic example to me is the software preferences window. That's where we tweak an application until it looks and works in just the right way for our needs. It's critical for our ability to pay attention and do work in an application that we find the right settings. But that's precisely why it's so easy to get trapped in there for hours fiddling around instead of getting anything done.

At some point, we have to stop tweaking and start living, and that takes dedication. If we're dedicated to building good relationships, doing good work, and living good lives, we have to be committed to the practice of returning to that calling in the ever-present moment. Mindfulness gives us that foundation of commitment. We have to set up our external *and* internal technologies in ways that support each other.

<<<< JOURNALING >>>>

I've always kept a journal. If the word "journalist" ever honestly applied to me, it was to mean "one who journals," not "one who does journalism." Journaling helps me cope. In order to deal with a day, I have to write down what happened, look at it, and then try to make sense of it. Journaling is a more natural tool for a human brain than fire. It's a fundamentally different technique from writing to communicate information or to express oneself to others. Journaling is a way to freeze and examine the contents of one's own mind, and the insight to be gained from that is invaluable. "The habit of writing for my eye only is good practice," Virginia Woolf wrote. "It loosens the ligaments."[7]

So in the interest of the species, I've tried to make journaling into a mission. I published much of my journaling for a while, but that didn't work. I couldn't speak freely. I had to tailor what I wrote to be more legible—not to mention polite—to outsiders, even if they were close friends or family. Maybe especially for them. I also took jobs blogging on large platforms. But my blogging career broke apart the well-tested journaling format I had developed my whole life.

Instead of my beautiful books—their purposes defined entirely by my own web of meanings that reached into and throughout their contents—I was cramming my journal entries into content management systems that spat them out into websites designed for browsing and—much worse—advertising. I was feeding the beast, blogging into the yawning vortex of new content posted online every day and irradiating people's attention spans. And because of the nature of the business, I never got to stop and reflect. Writing for a web publication hurt my attention span, and I'm afraid it hurt my readers' attention spans, too.

A perspective is only legible in the context of its

native person. I moved the vast majority of my journaling back into private, and everything made sense again. I was back on the road toward understanding my life. Mindfulness became possible again, and I could better see my thoughts in the context of my ongoing life patterns. I realized that journaling was more meaningful to me as a private process. On the other hand, the products of journaling—any insights or significant key turns of phrase—could be extracted and put into service to help others.

For the past few years—even through the periods of neglect—my private journal has been computerized. I use a journal app, Day One, that syncs between my phone and my computer, and it feels as personal as any paper book in which I've written, but it's much more powerful. I've done some of my life's best journaling in there. Now, when I have to write on paper, I treat those journals as drafts, and I either transcribe the pages or just photograph them and keep them in the app. When I feel like writing or drawing by hand for artistic reasons, I snap a nice photo of that work and put it into the digital journal, too.

Sometimes a personal observation is helped by feedback. It needs corroboration or refutation to feel meaningful. Despite its compromises, journaling on the web offers this. Day One lets you selectively publish pages to the web as beautiful stand-alone web pages so anyone can read them. If there's an image attached, it displays in high resolution at the top. It's not a blog, though. It's just a single page of the journal that stands on its own, which one can share to social networks or anywhere else on the web. This provides the best of both worlds. Any page of the journal that might bring about a meaningful connection with others can be easily shared. The rest of the journal remains perfectly private, which is the essential quality of journaling that makes it so liberating.

I still only keep one journal. It's almost entirely private. In fact, it's locked behind a password. But when I choose, I can turn one page outward, putting it on the web to receive feedback from humanity. I can gather feedback for my observation; and from my perspective, it is integrated with my journal. From the perspective of others, it's a slice of time from someone else's journal. It's a gesture of vulnerability and openness. A real act of sharing. A meaningful check-in about how someone is doing. My inner world can feel like an isolated, lonely place. So I share pages from time to time, and it makes me feel connected.

My point is not that software journals are better than paper ones. My point is that it's the *practices* encouraged by one's medium that matter, not the medium itself. Honestly, if I had a digital journal that was the perfect journal, but it didn't have any other apps, I would use it.

There are advantages of analog journals that I do miss, like the inability to multitask, which is a tempting distraction when journaling on my phone. That limited focus of paper is a feature, not a bug, as they say in the software business. There's also evidence to suggest that the motor skills employed in longhand writing aid learning and memory, so I really hope for improvements in the realism of stylus-based digital writing.[8] In the meantime, I sometimes just write by hand on paper because it feels good. I even like the inability to delete handwritten words sometimes, though on balance I think I prefer to have the option. But it's not the objective superiority of one kind of journaling or another that matters. It's journaling itself, the act of reflecting creatively on one's state of mind, that matters. Whatever journaling technology best encourages you to do that is the one you should use, and that's entirely up to you.

<<<< DOING YOUR CHORES >>>>

It's not all fun and games. Sometimes you have to do your chores. Nobody likes tidying up their desk, but eventually you have to do it. You get to the point where you can't find anything you need underneath all the stuff, so you make a Herculean effort and clean it all up, at which point the clock resets to zero, and you start making piles again.

That's how it is with physical desks. With most people's computers, that's what it's like on the best of all possible days. Most of the time, because the stuff in the piles isn't physically in the way, it just keeps piling up forever. Yes, you can search your computer for what you're looking for, magically slicing through the piles of mess. That will work for a while. But then your disk gets full, everything slows down, and you might even think you need a whole new computer, just because the mess got so out of control.

"Workflow" is an industry term for the procedure by which you do a job, describing the steps taken with each tool. Usually, thinking about workflows is pretty geeky. In fact, good user experience designers try not to make people notice the workflows for doing what they need to do at all. But mindfulness of our workflows shows us whether or not a tool is serving us well. We may not be very picky about good workflows, but we should at least notice when one is driving us crazy. And that's the starting point for becoming more sensitized to good user experience design.

And lest you think this is getting too geeky too quickly, I propose the idea that attention to workflow is a totally spiritual value. As we've discussed, there are more technologies in our lives than just our computers. Even the modes and tools of thought in our minds can be considered technologies. Correspondingly, there are workflows involved in the way we use these tools, and thus how we deal with many aspects of our lives.

For instance, let's consider the technology of mindfulness. Mindfulness is a technology we apply to help us stay focused on our highest work. Our typical mindfulness workflow is not very good. We go about our business getting distracted and stressed out, getting emotionally worked up, and letting that bias our attention. We forget to check in with our mindfulness, which would help us stay focused on what is instead of getting lost in illusions.

But if we practice meditation, we develop a much better workflow. Every day, we practice meditation for a few minutes. Meditation has a very familiar workflow. Sit in your posture, then start the timer or wait for the bell. Get settled and grounded into your posture. Once you're settled, begin to notice your breathing. Watch the breath as it comes in. Watch the breath as it goes out. Continue doing this. When you get distracted, just notice your mind wandering and bring it back to the breath. Just keep bringing your attention back over and over. That's the practice. These sound like the verbal instructions of a meditation teacher, don't they? That's because meditation, though it has the highest spiritual impact, is basically a practical activity. That's why we call it practice.

Meditation has a workflow, and we practice it to make it familiar. We practice because this workflow lets us engage our mindfulness more strongly and easily, so we can leave it running while we go about our day. Then, each time we get distracted, we notice, we note it to ourselves without judgment, and we return our attention to the present moment. This is basic stuff for mindfulness practitioners, but it may not have occurred to you that it's actually a pretty geeky workflow.

Maintaining a good mindfulness workflow is important for the jobs you do with your mind. Maintaining good software workflows is just as important for the jobs you do with your computer. Since those, too, are spiritual jobs, the workflows are sacred, even if they're geeky.

Imagine your dream desk. There's nothing on the surface except the tools you use to get things done. A closed laptop. A warm lamp. Blank paper. A blue pen, a black pen, and a red pen. That's it. No piles of documents. No mugs with damp tea bags in them. No tangled cables. No dust. Everything is in place for you to just sit down and get to work. Doesn't that sound calming and inspiring?

Now open the lid of the dream laptop and look at the screen. Do you see piles of icons all over the desktop, an overflowing trash, a stuffed downloads folder, five or ten open windows, all kinds of applications running simultaneously, pop-ups everywhere telling you to update things? Is that what using a computer feels like? If so, you aren't imagining hard enough.

What if, when you opened the laptop, the working environment was as immaculate as the desk? There's nothing on the desktop except the project you're actively working on. Only the applications you need every day are visible, ready to launch, but they're closed. Everything's emptied out and up to date. There are no pop-ups anywhere. You can go straight to work without undue stress or distraction.

This state of readiness is considered so desirable—and yet so unattainable—that popular culture has taken to calling it "Zen," as though it's some kind of exalted, enlightened state. There's something so funny about that to me. It's as though the highest teaching of Zen Buddhism is to have a clean floor, not a clean mind. But the computer, the desk, and the mind are all continuous. They all need to be disciplined in order to accomplish anything. The bottom line is that a little clean-up before working on something will save you *tons* of work during and after. And if we're prepared to do the spiritual work behind our everyday work, then our clean workspaces will serve those higher purposes.

Whether your tool is the computer or the cushion, doing the work has to start with inward discipline and preparedness. That means making the time to stay away from distractions, to recharge our spiritual batteries, and to practice meditation. It also means bringing that practice into the world with us, so we can recharge and recover in small ways throughout our everyday lives.

Similarly, we can set up our virtual environments to be much less distracting, so that they promote mindfulness and ways of working that are mentally and physically healthier. We can arrange our tools in ways that allow our minds to wander all over the place, or we can set them so that attention is resting on the body, in the present moment, on what really needs to be done.

Meditation practice is critical to staying healthy and balanced while out in the world. But it's also important to see how the setup of one's tech tools can make a huge difference. Your distractions can be right under the surface, waiting for you to stumble past, so they can pounce on you, with your browser that you specifically opened, with all of its enticing and distracting tabs. Or, knowing how much you love to get sucked into Facebook wormholes, and other online rabbit holes and rat holes, you can set up your workspace to avoid them, log out and delete apps ahead of time, resist temptation, and focus on what really matters.

I think there's widespread confusion about the reason digital technology gets blamed for distracting us. The problem is not that tech creates unnatural interruptions.

As we know from our meditation practice, there are always interruptions available to us. If there's nothing in our external environment to distract us, oh, our minds will surely come up with something. That's the mind's nature. The problem tech causes is that it's too good at indulging our nature, so we have to balance our relationship with it, just like we do with our food.

As we covered earlier, it's in the business interests of many technology companies to give us too much of a good thing. Social media apps, for example, provide us the same rewards as primate social grooming behaviors have done since the dawn of time. When handled appropriately, these rewards keep us sociable and sane. But when you put social grooming on the Internet, it's within reach at all times, and when you pump it full of desperation by supporting it with advertising, it becomes this addictive time suck. So if we want to use that natural reward as a motivator, we have to be disciplined. If we can't be disciplined enough to use this reward moderately, we have to find a different one.

The hard part, as always, is paying enough attention to keep these tempting forces under control. We have to notice when we're going down the social media rabbit hole. We have to catch ourselves when our mind is wandering. This is the hard part, and it just takes practice. There's only so much we can do to control our external environment. Beyond that, meditation practice is all we've got.

But notice how much easier we can make that challenge by implementing the right technologies—and avoiding the wrong ones—in the right ways. We are the designers of our own systems of living. We can design them to support our practice. Meditation is a powerful technology because it's not just one program. It's a foundation that underlies everything we do. We can build and rebuild our entire way of living and working to support our practice.

<<<< STAYING AT THE LEARNING EDGE >>>>

The particular mix of technologies you need and use for spiritual work will change. The contemporary state of technology will change, and the work you do will change. The foundation for a spiritual relationship with technology is not expertise in specific technologies. Rather, it's a methodology, or a practice if you prefer. It's a way of seeing, doing, and learning. It's a mindset.

The surface layer of that mindset is the understanding of work and jobs to be done that this book is intended to cultivate. It means not losing sight of the job any piece of technology—digital, analog, or mental—is doing for you, and remembering that it's only doing that job because you hired it. This requires a practice of reflecting often on the question: *What is your work?* By reorienting ourselves regularly towards the most meaningful goals, we begin the process of breaking down what we need to do next into actionable chunks. Then we can assess what technologies we need to complete those actions. But in doing so, we have to practice not losing sight of our work and our sense of purpose and meaning. That's the part of the mindset that's below the surface.

The inner layer of the mindset is mindfulness of *how* we're doing our work and the effect it's having on us. That part requires introspection, which gives us the insight we need to live a healthy high-tech life and leads to the compassion we need to help create a healthier world for others. Many of us are taught to rush, to work hard, and to keep busy. Introspection isn't practiced or encouraged. To commit to turning inward requires both a diligence and, paradoxically, a community of others committed to practice. We need to see the way we want to live reflected all around us, not just as an ideal within. That's the benefit of committing with a small group of others to, for example, spend a little time each week or each day sitting quietly together.

It's possible that the early generations of people inundated with mobile and Internet-connected digital technologies will never develop a mature relationship with them. We may never be able to fully concentrate on using our technology to do only work that feels spiritually fulfilling in our hearts. But at least we can encourage the next generation differently.

Appeals about saving the world for the next generation are commonplace. But this goal is attainable. It's not an ends-focused tirade, just a practical change in means. We can hope the result of a better world shakes out of it. Let's not present the next generation with digital technology as simply a source of entertainment. Let's show them technology as another surface of the world around them, one they can see through into hidden realms. Let's get away from the lesson that "screen time" is some tantalizing escape that makes children long for it. Let's show them how technology is an extension of themselves. Let's trust our children to come up with their own answers to our encouraging question: *What are you doing in this moment?*

It's not too late for us, either. Remember that the attention economy goes bankrupt if we starve it of attention. It's designed to suck us back in, but we can resist. We can bring our attention back to our real work, where both real joy and connection are to be found. It just takes practice.

ACKNOWLEDGMENTS

To my grandparents, Barbara and Lloyd Kupferberg and Arlene and Mayer Mitchell, who all taught me in their own ways to connect with the wisdom of my ancestors.

To my parents, Susan Kupferberg and Richard Mitchell, who encouraged me to pursue my curiosity in any direction it led me.

To Joseph Walsh, my first spiritual teacher in high school, who taught me that miracles are ordinary.

To Hal Roth and Willoughby Britton, who showed me that it is worthy to study the inner life.

To Randall Leeds, who showed me that language is politics in code.

To Will Chase, who saw some holy spark in my writing and gave me the outlet to write about the human spirit alongside the cold metal of Silicon Valley.

To all the editors I've ever had.

To Micah Daigle, who pushed me into the joyous free-fall of a career change that opened me up to my life's work.

To Glenn Fleishman, who gave me the interview that served as the diving board into this book.

And to Ariel Root Wolpe, rabbi-to-be, whose spiritual leadership and loving companionship will be my moon in the sky, the guide of my work from now on.

NOTES

CHAPTER ONE: SPIRITUAL WORK, SPIRITUAL JOBS

1. Debbie Millman, *Look Both Ways: Illustrated Essys on the Intersection of Life and Design* (Cinvcinnati, OH: HOW Books, 2009).

2. David Allen, *Getting Things Done* (New York: Penguin, 2002).

3. David Allen, *Ready for Anything* (New York: Penguin, 2004).

4. Alain de Botton, "On Distraction," City Journal (Spring 2012): http://www.city-journal.org/2010/20_2_snd-concentration.html.

CHAPTER TWO: WHAT IS TECHNOLOGY?

1. Kevin Kelly, *What Technology Wants* (New York: Penguin, 2010).

2. Ibid.

3. Ibid.

4. Ibid.

5. Ibid.

CHAPTER THREE: TECHNOLOGY AND SPIRITUALITY

1. Nathan Jurgenson, "The IRL Fetish." The New Inquiry (June 2012): http://thenewinquiry.com/essays/the-irl-fetish/.

2. Ibid.

3. Jon Kabat-Zinn, Wherever You Go, There You Are: Mindfulness Meditation in Everyday Life (New York: Hyperion, 1994).

4, Amanda Hess, "Why Women Aren't Welcome on the Internet," Pacific Standard (January/February 2014): http://www.psmag.com/navigation/health-and-behavior/women-arent-welcome-internet-72170/.

5. Chris Mooney, "The Science of Why Comment Trolls Suck,"

Mother Jones (January 2013): http://www.motherjones.com/environment/2013/01/you-idiot-course-trolls-comments-make-you-believe-science-less.

6. Ryuel, "The Buddha's Teaching on Right Speech," Fraught with Peril (April 2012): http://fraughtwithperil.com/ryuel/2012/04/01/the-buddhas-teaching-on-right-speech/.

CHAPTER FOUR: THE MAGIC AND THE MAYHEM

1. Chögyam Trungpa, *Cutting Through Spiritual Materialism* (Boston, MA: Shambhala, 2002), 210.

2. Arthur C. Clarke, *Profiles of the Future: An Inquiry into the Limits of the Possible* (London: Orion Publishing, 2000).

3. Ashley Vance, "This Tech Bubble Is Different," *Bloomberg Businessweek Magazine* (April 2011): http//www.businessweek.com/printer/articles/55578-this-tech-bubble-is-different.

4. Ibid.

5. Jaron Lanier, *You Are Not a Gadget: A Manifesto* (New York: Alfred A. Knopf, 2010).

6. Cory Doctorow, "The NSAs Prism: Why We Should Care," The Guardian (June 2013): http://www.theguardian.com/technology/blog/2013/jun/14/nsa-prism.

7. Trungpa Rinpoche, *Cutting Through Spiritual Materialism*.

8. Lan Anh Nguyen, "Exclusive: Flappy Bird Creator Dong Nguyen Says App 'Gone Forever' Because It Was 'An Addictive Product,'" Forbes (February 2013).

9. Seth Stevenson, "Mob Justice," Slate.com (March 2013): http://www.slate.com/articles/technology/the_browser/2013/03/karen_klein_bullied_bus_monitor_why_did_a_bunch_of_people_on_the_internet.html.

10. Masahiro Mori, "The Uncanny Valley," *IEEE Spectrum* (June 2012): http://spectrum.ieee.org/automaton/robotics/humanoids/the-uncanny-valley.

11. Ibid.

12. Ray Kurzweil, *The Age of Spiritual Machines: When Computers Exceed Human Intelligence* (Viking, 1999).

13. Ibid.

14. Adrianne Jeffries, "You're Not Going to Read This but You'll Probably Share It Anyway," TheVerge.com (February 2014): http: //www. theverge.com/2014/2/14/5411934/you're-not-going-to-read-this.

15. Nicholas Carr, *The Shallows: What the Internet Is Doing to Our Brains* (New York: W.W. Norton2010), 48.

16. Sharon Begley, *Train Your Mind, Change Your Brain* (New York: Ballantine Books, 2007), 217.

CHAPTER FIVE: BEHIND THE CURTAIN

1. Marshall Kirkpatrick, "Facebook's Zuckerberg Says the Age of Privacy Is Over," ReadWrite.com (January 2010) http://readwrite. com/2010/01/09/facebooks_zuckerberg_says_the_age_of_privacy_ is_ov.

2. Theodore Levitt, *The Marketing Imagination* (New York: Free Press, 1983).

3. Clayton Christenson and Micael E Raynor, *The Innovator's Solution: Creating and Sustaining Successful Growth* (Boston, MA: Harvard Business School Press, 2003).

4. Asymco.com can be found at http://www.asymco.com.

5. Horace Dediu, "Innoveracy: Misunderstanding Innovation, "Asymco. com (April 2014): http://www.asymco.com/2014/04/16/ innoveracy-misunderstanding-innovation/.

6. Rick Levine, Christopher Locke, Doc Searls, and David Weinberger, *The Cluetrain Manifesto: The End of Business as Usual* (Philadelphia, PA: Basic Books, 2009), xv.

CHAPTER SIX: HOW TO DISCONNECT

1. Kabat-Zinn, *Wherever You Go, There You Are.*

2. David Lynch, *Catching the Big Fish:Meditation, Consciousness, and Creativity* (New York: Tarcher/Penguin, 2007).

3. Carlos Greg Diuk, "The Formation of Love," Facebook.com (February 2014): https://www.facebook.com/notes/facebook-data-science/the-formation-of-love/10152064609253859.

4. "Louis C.K. Hates Cell Phones," YouTube video, 4:50, from an episode of Conan, posted by "Team Coco," September 20, 2013, https://www.youtube.com/watch?v=5HbYScltf1c.

5. Joel Lovell, "George Saunders's Advice to Graduates," NYTimes.com (July2013): http://6thfloor.blogs.nytimes.com/2013/07/31/george-saunderss-advice-to-graduates/?_php=true&_r=1&pagewanted=all.

6. Kabat-Zinn, *Wherever You Go, There You Are*, 35.

7. Larry Harvey, "Commerce & Community: Distilling Philosophy from a Cup of Coffee," Blog.BurningMan.com (November 2013): http://blog.burningman.com/2013/11/tenprinciples/commerce-community-distilling-philosophy-from-a-cup-of-coffee/.

8. Larry Harvey, "Introduction: The Philosophical Center," Blog.BurningMan.com (November 2013): https://blog.burningman.com/2013/11/tenprinciples/introduction-the-philosophical-center/.

9. Emily Witt, "Diary," *London Review of Books* vol. 36, no 14 (17 July 2014): http://www.lrb.co.uk/v36/n14/emily-witt/diary.

CHAPTER SEVEN: SPIRITUAL PRACTICES

1. Abraham Joshua Heschel, *The Sabbath* (New York: Farrar, Straus and Giroux, 2005).

2. Alan Lightman, *Einstein's Dreams* (New York: Warner Books, 1994).

3. Norman Waddell and Masao Abe, *The Heart of Dōgen's Shōbōgenzō* (Albany, NY: SUNY Press, 2002).

4. Kabat-Zinn, *Wherever You Go, There You Are.*

5. Omori Sogen, *An Introduction to Zen Training.*

6. Trungpa Rinpoche, *Cutting Through Spiritual Materialism.*

7. Virginia Woolf, quoted in Maria Popova, "Virginia Woolf on the Creative Benefits of Keeping a Diary," BrainPickings.org (January 2013): http://www.brainpickings.org/2013/01/25/virginia-woolf-on-keeping-a-diary/.

8. Maria Konnikova, "What's Lost as Handwriting Fades," *The New York Times* (3 June 2014): http://www.nytimes.com/2014/06/03/science/whats-lost-as-handwriting-fades.html?pagewanted=all.

REFERENCES

These are texts that informed and inspired what I wrote. Some of them are quoted directly in various places in this book. Others are formative works I read a long time ago that shaped my thinking on questions of spirituality, mindfulness, and technology. Before I name them, this is an acknowledgment that few of these texts were written by women. I want to make clear that this is not a definitive list of texts on these topics, only the list of the ones with which I've happened to cross paths so far. I look forward with great anticipation to extending this list to works by women, and I believe fervently in correcting the disparity in empowered voices along gender lines.

Allen, David. *Getting Things Done: The Art of Stress-Free Productivity*. New York: Viking, 2001.

Carr, Nicholas G. *The Shallows: What the Internet Is Doing to Our Brains*. New York: W.W. Norton, 2010.

Csikszentmihalyi, Mihaly. *Flow: The Psychology of Optimal Experience.* New York: Harper & Row, 1990.

Heschel, Abraham Joshua. *The Sabbath, Its Meaning for Modern Man.* New York: Farrar, Straus and Young, 1951.

Jurgensen, Nathan. "The Disconnectionists." *The New Inquiry*. http://thenewinquiry.com/essays/the-disconnectionists/ (accessed September 14, 2014).

Kabat-Zinn, Jon. *Wherever You Go, There You Are: Mindfulness Meditation in Everyday Life.* New York: Hyperion, 1994.

Kelly, Kevin. *What Technology Wants.* New York: Viking, 2010.

Lanier, Jaron. *You Are Not a Gadget: A Manifesto.* New York: Alfred A. Knopf, 2010.

Lightman, Alan P. *Einstein's Dreams.* New York: Pantheon Books, 1993.

Mann, Merlin. *Inbox Zero: Cutting through the Crap to Do the Work That Matters.* New York: Harper Business, 2012.

Pirsig, Robert M. *Zen and the Art of Motorcycle Maintenance: An Inquiry into Values.* New York: Morrow, 1974.

Rushkoff, Douglas. *Present Shock: When Everything Happens Now.* New York: Current, 2013.

Trungpa, Chögyam. *Cutting through Spiritual Materialism.* Berkeley: Shambhala, 1973.

Turkle, Sherry. *Alone Together: Why We Expect More from Technology and Less from Each Other.* New York: Basic Books, 2012.

Victor, Bret. A Brief Rant on the Future of Interaction Design. http://worrydream.com/ABriefRantOnTheFutureOfInteractionDesign/ (accessed September 14, 2014).

ABOUT THE AUTHOR

Jon Mitchell has worked as a journalist for ReadWrite.com and several other web publications. He is the managing editor for Burning Man, and has recorded a rock album called *Portal*. Mitchell lives in Los Angeles, California.

RELATED TITLES
FROM PARALLAX PRESS

Awakening Joy
James Baraz and Shoshana Alexander

Good Citizens
Thich Nhat Hanh

Happiness
Thich Nhat Hanh

How to Sit
Thich Nhat Hanh

Love Letter to the Earth
Thich Nhat Hanh

The Mindfulness Survival Kit
Thich Nhat Hanh

Not Quite Nirvana
Rachel Neumann

Solid Ground
Sylvia Boorstein, Norman Fischer, Tsoknyi Rinpoche

Ten Breaths to Happiness
Glen Schneider

Work
Thich Nhat Hanh

PARALLAX
PRESS

Parallax Press is a nonprofit publisher, founded and inspired by Zen Master Thich Nhat Hanh. We publish books on mindfulness in daily life and are committed to making these teachings accessible to everyone and preserving them for future generations. We do this work to alleviate suffering and contribute to a more just and joyful world.

For a copy of the catalog, please contact:

Parallax Press

P.O. Box 7355

Berkeley, CA 94707

Tel: (510) 525-0101

parallax.org

PARALLAX
PRESS

Parallax Press, a nonprofit organization, publishes books on engaged Buddhism and the practice of mindfulness by Thich Nhat Hanh and other authors. All of Thich Nhat Hanh's work is available at our online store and in our free catalog. For a copy of the catalog, please contact:

Parallax Press
P.O. Box 7355
Berkeley, CA 94707
Tel: (510) 525-0101
parallax.org

Monastics and laypeople practice the art of mindful living in the tradition of Thich Nhat Hanh at retreat communities worldwide. To reach any of these communities, or for information about individuals and families joining for a practice period, please contact:

Plum Village
13 Martineau
33580 Dieulivol, France
plumvillage.org

Blue Cliff Monastery
3 Mindfulness Road
Pine Bush, NY 12566
bluecliffmonastery.org

Magnolia Grove Monastery
123 Towles Rd.
Batesville, MS 38606
magnoliagrovemonastery.org

Deer Park Monastery
2499 Melru Lane
Escondido, CA 92026
deerparkmonastery.org

The Mindfulness Bell, a journal of the art of mindful living in the tradition of Thich Nhat Hanh, is published three times a year by Plum Village. To subscribe or to see the worldwide directory of Sanghas, visitmindfulnessbell.org.